ROAD SCHOLARS

20 YEARS OF GETTING SCHOOLED BY THE SILK ROAD

Devotional Readings

by

DAN M KRULL
&
DINA M KRULL

Merry Christmas
Steve + Jill !
May the lord continue
to touch lives through you ♡
Love -
Dan + Dina

Cover Photo by Guillem Lopez
https://www.guillemlopez.com/index

WHAT PEOPLE ARE SAYING ABOUT *ROAD SCHOLARS...*

Since the fall of the Soviet Union, Dan and I have worked on projects together in Ukraine, Central Asia, and Turkey. In *Road Scholars*, Dan and Dina demonstrate how ordinary, available people can help change the nations.
Josh McDowell - Author, speaker

Dan and Dina's book on their journey through the Silk road is both real, raw, and dripping with insight and humor. Without a doubt, the best book I have read this year.
Al Goff - President & CEO Global Aid Network

I loved this book! The Krulls vulnerably and humbly guide us through the joys and sorrows of life on the Silk Road, while reminding us to find God and His signposts everywhere. As you read these tender stories, perhaps through tears, you will be inspired to love and serve.
Karen Cartmell - Spiritual Director, Talbot Seminary

Life is a journey; take something along to read! The Krull's journal will become your traveling companion; pour yourself a cup and change your day!
Bob Shank - Founder/CEO, The Master's Program

In *Road Scholars* Dan and Dina Krull capture the fun and frustration of cross-cultural living while calling us to a practical, biblical theology. Love it!
Dr. Ken Cochrum - Vice President, Global Digital Strategies for Cru

Dan and Dina Krull in their devotional book *Road Scholars* take us on a 28-day mission trip around the world. As I read each day's story, I was there! I could "see, smell, and experience" life abroad. Walk for 28 days with Dan and Dina and let Jesus change your life. You'll be glad you did.
Dr. Paul Friesen –Director Home Improvement Ministries, Author of *The Marriage App*

Some develop insight through study; others by being there. So, when Dina and Dan, having both studied and been there, share their story it's worth a thoughtful read.
Ansel Condray - Chairman and Production Director, Retired, ExxonMobil International, Ltd

Dan and Dina Krull open both their lives and the Scriptures to us in strikingly artistic, practical and effective ways through this devotional. This makes the book both enjoyable and life-changing. I highly recommend it as a resource for enriching both our understanding and communion with God.
Dr. Dela Adadevoh – President, International Leadership Foundation

In captivating current stories and related biblical reflections Dan and Dina share how God stripped away the superficial shell of modern comfortable Christianity from their lives in order to show them and us what it truly means to follow Christ and love others in today's broken world.
Rev. Jim Bzdafka - Senior Pastor, Providence Church

A lot of truth with a light touch--a real delight!
Erick Schenkel PhD - Executive Director, Jesus Film Project

Road Scholars is exquisite, mixing humor with sometimes heart wrenching stories that demonstrate the mysterious and awesome power of God in people's lives. This devotional will take you places you would never go on your own. Highly, highly recommended!

Pastor Dan Schaeffer - author of *The Better Country, The Power of Weakness* and *In Search of the Real Spirit of Christmas*.

After having done two tours in the former Soviet Union while in the Foreign Service, I can relate to Dan and Dina's daily life experiences...the Holy Spirit is shining his light in my life and saying "Hmm, maybe there is something you should think about here."

Daniel Thompson - Retired Foreign Service Specialist

Dan and Dina give texture and details that make these stories come to life!

Brian Boone - Senior Pastor, Community Christian Fellowship, Edmonds, WA

Dan and Dina Krull are some of the most "spiritual" people that I know. I am sure their example will increase your own desire to know Christ more and to be part of what He is doing in this world. This is a wonderful book!

Steve Calagna – Senior Pastor, North County Christian Fellowship

It doesn't get any more real than this. With candor, heart, and a lot of faith Dan and Dina offer us genuine insight and hope from having really been there. It's hard to find two people more innovative, and passionate in bring the hope of Jesus to the far reaches of our world.

Glenn Barteau Jr, - Senior Pastor of Casas Church/Surfer

In this collection of captivating personal stories of faith and adventure, Dan and Dina will invite you to experience God's extraordinary work through ordinary people of faith.

Dr. Bekele Shanko – VP Global Church Movements Cru/ Chairman GACX

This book dispels the glamour of missions' work and shows a picture of true life overseas.

Krissy Krull – Really smart 11th grader

Humorous and Inspiring

Ellie Krull – Yet another really smart 11th grader

DEDICATION

This book is dedicated to the hundreds of men and women who have given
of themselves to support our family over the past 25 years.
Our prayer is that these stories would showcase
how God has multiplied your gifts.

May the lives and lessons on these pages give you a tiny glimpse
of the work in which you have invested.
Thank you for not burying your treasure. Instead, you partnered with us by
faith, not knowing if there would be a measurable outcome.
Thank you for reaching out to embrace the people of
Persia, Central Asia and Turkey.

We also dedicate these pages to our four children –
Jack, Levi, Ellie and Krissy,
who have graciously adapted to our ever-changing lives.
You have filled our home with joy and laughter.
Your lives are priceless treasures that have brought
warmth and gladness to a broken world.
Wherever the future leads, may you always find your home in God Himself.

MAP OF THE ANCIENT SILK ROAD

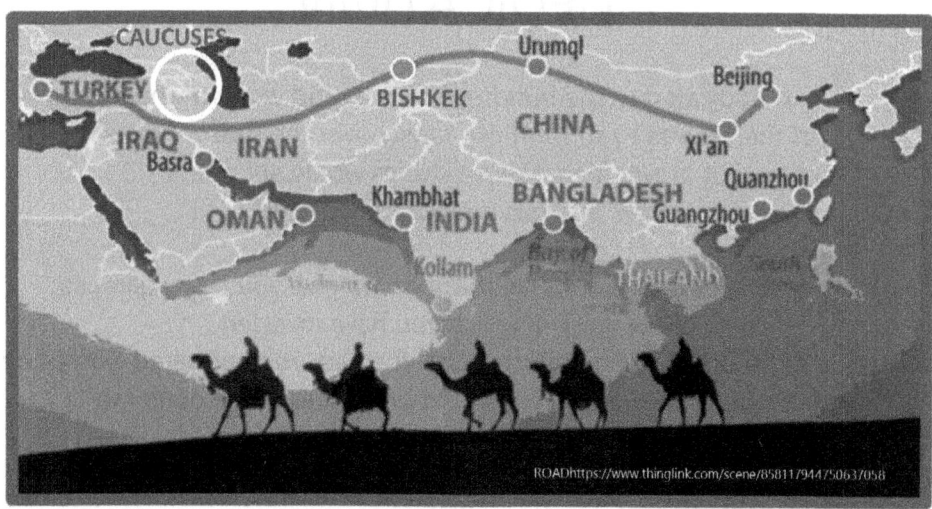

The Silk Road was an ancient network of trade routes that were central to cultural interaction through regions of Eurasia connecting the East and West and stretching from China to the Mediterranean Sea.

https://en.wikipedia.org/wiki/Silk_Road

CONTENTS

PREFACE...9

MONET VS. THE METRO..11

WHERE THE RUBBER MEETS THE ROAD LESS TRAVELLED 15

GOD'S CALLING FOR DUMMIES 21

STAR GIRL...27

HAPPY TRAILS 32

GREAT EXPECTATIONS 37

BUMBLE BEE 42

DREAM ON..47

TALE OF TWO NEIGHBORS 53

IT COULD BE ME...58

BARNYARD EQ 63

MUMFORD AND SONS 67

THE BOXER 72

FOCUS..78

WEDDING PARTY 85

BABOS...89

PORTABLE HOLIDAY 96

TWO TRUTHS AND A LIE..101

THE CORE EVENT 106

CINDERELLA 111

THE LITTLE GREEN BOOK 117

SAUTÉED RED ONION 123

THE TEST...129

CHOOSE THE MIDDLE SEAT 135

WAITING FOR THE BLUE ZONE..140

PARASITES AND MEDIOCRITY 146

I STILL HAVEN'T FOUND WHAT I'M LOOKING FOR 151

THE TREASURE 155

PREFACE

After 25 years in ministry, we took a two-month sabbatical hoping that God would instill refreshment and renewed direction into our lives. In the mid-1990s we embarked on a ten-year adventure of trying to exhibit the love of Jesus in Central Asia, followed by a five-year experiment with business as an avenue for influence in the Caucuses, north of Iran. The journey has been both exhilarating and demanding as we have shifted between continents and cultures while trying to preserve both family and friends. The years have stretched us all, which made this sabbatical timely and vital.

Only a few days into our downtime, we began to meditate on the parallel accounts of sabbath rest in the ten commandments.

Exodus 20:8-11	Deuteronomy 5:12-15
[8] "Remember to observe the Sabbath day by keeping it holy... [11] For in six days the LORD made the heavens, the earth, the sea, and everything in them; but on the seventh day he rested. That is why the LORD blessed the Sabbath day and set it apart as holy.	[12] "Observe the Sabbath day by keeping it holy ... [15] Remember that you were once slaves in Egypt, but the LORD your God brought you out with his strong hand and powerful arm. That is why the LORD your God has commanded you to rest on the Sabbath day.

While the Exodus account calls for Sabbath obedience as imitation of God's own resting on the seventh day, Deuteronomy gives an alternate motivation for setting aside weekly time. Sabbath is time dedicated to remember -- to remember the past work of God in our lives.

So, we spent the sabbatical days in our lawn chairs listing the wonders God had performed, from monumental to subtle during our three decades of journeying with Jesus. As our divine appreciation grew, we both became convinced that sharing our global and spiritual journey might embolden others in their view of God and the world.

Reading Brother Lawrence's 400-year-old advice on *Practicing the Presence of God*, it occurred to us that the author was simply a kitchen worker at a medieval monastery. If this venerable father of the faith had not paused to record his thoughts, not only would he have remained an anonymous dishwasher, but four centuries of Christendom would not have benefited from his life-changing insights. Since we, too, have some dish washing experience, and the example of an ordinary old monk, we decided to record our encounters of divine handiwork, often disguised as everyday blunders.

May our adventures on the Silk Road remind readers that God can use ordinary people to promote His purposes.

Enjoy,

Dan Michael Krull & Dina Marie Krull

MONET VS. THE METRO

Day 1 – by Dan

> "Great is the LORD and most worthy of praise;
> his greatness no one can fathom.
> One generation commends your works to another;
> they tell of your mighty acts.
> They speak of the glorious splendor of your majesty—
> and I will meditate on your wonderful works."
> Ps 145:3-5

For a year in the early '90s I made my home in Kiev, Ukraine. I spent most of my time learning Russian, meeting college students in front of the scarlet-red coated main building of Kiev State University, and looking for cheese.

One autumn weekend, I decided to brave the 13-hour train ride to Moscow to explore the former Soviet Union's center of power. I invited Doctor Sasha to join me. Since all the Russian and Ukrainian men I knew were named Sasha, Slava, or Oleg, I affectionately created descriptor nicknames in order to differentiate them while talking to friends. There was Sweater Sasha (who always wore the same striped sweater), Little Sasha (who happened to be a few inches shorter than Big Sasha), and the protagonist of this tale, Doctor Sasha (who was a budding medical student). As part of Doctor Sasha's medical training, he was tasked with administering daily sobriety tests on all the subway drivers for the Kiev subway lines. In that part of the world, a subway is known as a metro, and metro drivers are known to drink on occasion.

After a dozen hours of sitting upright, Doctor Sasha and I arrived at the Kievsky train station in Moscow and descended to the adjacent metro station. Key word – descended. The tunnels for the Moscow metro were built at the cost of thousands of lives under Stalin's command, and they seem to be located at the intersection of the earth's crust and mantle.

As an unofficial member of the metro-driver mafia in Kiev, Sasha apparently commanded a degree of respect among the Moscow metro drivers as well; he sauntered up to the cockpit and casually asked if his American friend could drive the passenger-laden subway to the next stop. The characteristically apathetic communism-inspired drivers shrugged their shoulders as if to say, "Sure, why not?"

I climbed into the cold gray cabin the size of a public bathroom stall with accompanying smells. Three Russians huddled behind me and mumbled some instructions with a tone which communicated, "Do whatever you want, we don't care." So, after pushing a couple of faded green and red buttons, and throttling a metallic T-shaped bar full forward, we were off. I felt like an overgrown squeaky gopher, guided by roots of subterranean steel and sagging black cable.

The well-worn subway, inside and out, wasn't much to look at, but it was quite effective at its intended purpose – daily shuttling thousands of black-and-gray clothed comrades off to markets, schools, and vodka factories. And here I was, 100 meters underground piloting the vessel that made a world population center function properly. Well, at least function.

Let me diverge for a second. I spend a lot of time mulling over rational arguments about why I believe in God and the benefits thereof. Unfortunately, I spend much more time thinking than I do actually talking to others about those reasons; but, regardless, here is what I've come up with. I call it the "don't fight gravity" framework of theology. It goes like this...

- God is smarter than you are
- He made ferns, and nautilus shells, and initiated quantum physics and non-tangible forces such as gravity that make stuff work as it does.
- If you live by God's principles as laid out in the Bible, you are aligning yourself with the way things are meant to work -– therefore things in life tend to work out better. So, why fight gravity?

I was pretty satisfied with my logic-inspired theological conclusions. However, I recently learned that Jonathan Edwards called this approach to morality and ethics "common virtue." This sounds pretty good at first, but what Edwards means by "common virtue" is that you are doing the "right" things out of the same sinful motivations as those moral people who don't give God a second thought.

If I'm doing what is "right" because I want life to work out well for myself, the driving motivations are either fear (I'm afraid of screwing up my life, or afraid of losing control over my life) or pride (I need to keep my life in line, so I don't end up like those goofballs who have blown it). Oddly enough, these are the same motivations that drive the bulk of sinful behavior. My "don't fight gravity" Christian life is really just a dressed-up version of my old sinful self.

Edwards would say that common virtue isn't a bad thing, but it isn't true virtue either. It is an incomplete picture of God.[i] And if I obey God only out of self-centered fear or pride, even my moral motivation will eventually implode.

A.W. Tozer writes that, "The essence of idolatry is the entertainment of thoughts about God that are unworthy of Him," and, "we tend by a secret law of the soul to move toward our mental image of God."[ii]

Common virtue is an idea unworthy of God. It turns God into a means of transportation. God will get me where I want to go if I play according to His rules. But God wants to be more than that. He wants to be the beginning, middle, and end of my journey, not just the vehicle to get me to my own puny ends.

God is not like a Soviet subway – unattractive but effective in getting me where I want to go. God is like the Tretyakovsky Gallery, which is where the Moscow subway dropped me off that autumn day in 1991.

Inside the Tretyakovsky Art Gallery that year there was a series of paintings by Claude Monet depicting more than thirty views of Rouen Cathedral. The subtlety, color choice, and mastery of technique were mesmerizing. I stood staring for 20 minutes and felt like I could have stayed hours longer. The paintings serve no "other" purpose. They just hang there depicting beauty. I can't understand how Monet created such splendor, nor why he chose his subject matter. But I do know that such "useless" beauty is closer to who God is, than my utilitarian "don't fight gravity" view of Him.

Edwards defines true virtue as loving and obeying God because He is beautiful. God is compelling and holy and worthy. In true virtue, I obey not because it makes life work, not because it's rational, but because I stand in front of God, mesmerized by His beauty.

> "Great is the LORD and most worthy of praise;
> his greatness no one can fathom.
> One generation commends your works to another;
> they tell of your mighty acts.
> They speak of the glorious splendor of your majesty—
> and I will meditate on your wonderful works."
> Ps 145:3-5

REFLECTION

1. In what ways has following God's plan made your life more successful? (Josh 1:8)

2. What aspects of God's character do you admire most?

3. How might you grow in true virtue i.e. treasuring God for who He is, not only for what He provides?

WHERE THE RUBBER MEETS THE ROAD LESS TRAVELLED
Day 2 – by Dina

> "The plans of man are many, but the Lord's purpose will prevail"
> Proverbs 19:21

"Did you see the red flag when you flew in?" the tall, weathered taxi driver asked.

"You mean the Russian flag?" I commented, pointing to the waving striped cloth contrasted against the pale icy sky.

"Yes," he said, nodding.

"The red flag was a warning, didn't you realize?" Vladimir chuckled as a stream of cigarette smoke made its way through his gapped-toothed smile. I finally got the humor and took it to heart as I fought back the panic welling up within me.

Dan and I had sprinted to baggage claim and frantically sought a taxi driver to drive us one kilometer between the two Moscow airports, conveniently named Sheremetova #1 and Sheremetova #2. Our US travel agent had assured us countless times that we wouldn't need this transfer on our journey from San Francisco to Almaty, Kazakhstan, but since the two airports had the same name, no foreign travel agent or information booth worker could tell the difference. So upon arrival, with only 45 minutes to connect to our Russia-Kazakhstan connecting flight at a different airport, we were in a hurry.

After a panic-stricken half-hour of juggling our 4 army-surplus bags to the dirty white Volga sedan in the parking lot, we sped to Shermetova #2, only to find out that our flight had been canceled due to airport closure. War had broken out in Chechnya, and the Russian Army had commandeered the airport to stage its retaliation. The midnight sky was busy with air activity, but none of it was going the direction we wanted.

Twenty hours earlier, back in the USA, we had said our "goodbyes." We were ready to get on with our mission...but we hadn't even gotten to our destination, and the honeymoon stage was already over.

My stormy whirlwind of thoughts began to multiply as I realized we would not show up on our "scheduled" flight, and we hadn't come up with plan "B" or "C." Though we had friends in Moscow, neither Dan nor I had thought of getting their contact information, not to mention the phone numbers of our counterparts in Almaty, Kazakhstan, who were making their way to the airport to meet us. *What were we thinking...?* I thought. No plan, no clever ideas. Hadn't my husband lived in this city before? Yes, but we hadn't anticipated the cessation of airline activity nor had we entered the age of mobile phones that have all contact information stored in their tidy little pocket-sized bundles. But he did remember that there was an international hotel near the airport.

Dan blurted out to our driver, "Do you know the Novotel?"

"Sure," Vladimir replied.

We directed him to take us to the hotel, thinking perhaps we could stay the night, pull ourselves together, and devise a plan forward. Upon arrival at Novotel, the bright shiny entry was inviting after the airport's mix of dim oppressive brown lighting, cigarette smoke, and sea of fur hats. We raced to the desk to see what they could offer our two lost souls.

"Two hundred dollars a night!"

In 1994, as a newlywed couple, we had just put everything we owned in the back of a Ford Ranger, sold our wedding gifts, and chose the "road less travelled", which came with "the road of less salary." Two hundred dollars was more than we could imagine paying for a place to re-group. We hung our heads and walked back to the taxi that held our life's belongings. Vladimir smirked and offered an option of his own.

"It's New Year's Eve, Why don't you just stay the night at my place?"

Fortunately, Dan had lived in Ukraine before we got married and his Russian language was good. He translated the offer after he had agreed on the arrangement. After a few horrible scenarios flashed through my mind, I decided, with fear and trembling, that I didn't have any other brilliant options of my own. On this frigid New Year's Eve, I guess we would have to entrust ourselves to this stranger with a half-saintly and half-mischievous demeanor. My guard valiantly wanted to be up, but I had no Russian skills to negotiate or investigate further. In addition, since my husband of two years had already accepted the stranger's invitation, I had no choice but to submit.

Kielbasa sizzled in the heavy pan as we squeezed into a kitchen "ugolnik"-- a corner bench that nudged up to a small table. Vladimir lined up some shot glasses and with his gapped-toothed smile began ringing in the New Year with his new-found friends. He didn't appear to care that we barely sipped as he gulped the Vodka. Olga had been jostled out of bed to get some food on the table. It didn't seem to be her first encounter with this type of thing. My head was spinning out of control with fatigue, confusion, and the humble position I found myself in -- at the mercy of two unknown Russians. As the shot glasses were lifted, Vladimir became louder and more jovial, laughter filled the air, occupying the space that the smoke from the frying sausage had yet to fill. Olga flopped the sausages on a plate before me. They slipped around in their grease, painting abstracts on my plate. Olga's XL bosom threatened to burst out of her housecoat. Her chest was the same shade of pink as the sausages before me and blended together in a fuzzy sort of way. My delirious state was getting the best of me.

After reluctantly sipping a shot of vodka through gritted teeth, poking at a salty lump of canned cabbage and the aforementioned oily chunks of processed meat, we were ushered into the front room, handed a blanket and pillow and welcomed to the couch. The room was dimly lit by the small decorated New Year's pine tree propped up on a nearby stool. With no answers, no plan, and no more capacity for thoughts to taunt me, I drifted away into a deep sleep.

Six hours later I awoke with a fresh set of ponderings. The unexpected had shown up as a villain in my well-rehearsed play. Weren't we the protagonists? Weren't we due some rewards for our hard-earned language learning, support raising, and sacrifice of family and possessions? Apparently not. Our plans were merely plans, not ultimate reality. My false assumption was that plans were not to be tampered with. Despite our grandiose intention of bringing hope to the hopeless on the other side of the world, I realized for the first time, I was not really the one in control.

Our original plane ticket disappeared in the Chechen conflict. The original itinerary was no longer a possibility for civilians. No matter how much I cried, worried, or wanted to complain, I realized I couldn't change the fact that war had broken out. An entire foreign government had no concern that I was inconvenienced. So, with Vladimir's help and a few phone calls, we discovered that an alternate flight was leaving the following day to Kazakhstan from a tiny airport on the opposite side of Moscow.

Upon arrival at the homely Domodedova airport, we fought off the luggage mafia who demanded $100 per bag to put our luggage on a cart from the car to the terminal (which looked like a prison barracks). One by one, Dan shuttled our 70 pound bags to the check-in desk, while I waited with Vladimir to make sure none of our precious cargo went missing. We finally found a window that decided it had two tickets for their evening flight to Almaty, Kazakhstan.

After buying new tickets, we gave our Good Samaritan Vladimir the rest of the cash we had on us. Riding on the merciful wave of God's grace, we parted ways with Moscow and crossed into Asia. It was as if angels lifted us from one place to another to bring our weary bodies where they needed to be.

But where exactly was that? On the next leg of our journey from Kazakhstan to Kyrgyzstan, I shuffled my feet on the gritty floor as I stared off into the distance through the van's tarnished window. My solace was found in a half-eaten bag of Wheat Thins I had shoved into my purse upon departure in San Francisco. The salty wafers were inexplicably comforting. To this day, I'm amazed how close to my heart they became. I hated to throw the wrapper away, as if I had just let go of the only friend I felt I knew.

Two hours into the lifeless steppe of Kazakhstan, I spotted a yurt. There it was -- the National Geographic photo moment journalists travel far and wide to get. I didn't really care at that point because I desperately had to go to the bathroom and began to dread how that would all take place. Dan communicated to the driver that a stop was inevitable for us. The driver shook his head and rattled off a few sentences. Within a couple of kilometers, we were told that "the peeing bear" would appear. I questioned my husband's translation, but he confirmed that is what the driver said. "Did you tell him I needed a restroom? Not a bear?"

Dan began to disregard my questions. So the one-way dialogue soon ceased, and I felt my eyes well up with tears. Before I could get myself too worked up, the van rolled to a stop in front of several shish-kabob stands loosely arranged around a large statue of what looked like a peeing bear. On each of the coal-filled steel boxes sat skewers of lamb meat, horse meat, and sizzling fat. The driver looked at me and pointed to a wall. I guessed that this was my point of destination.

Sure enough, I rounded the wall to find four elderly women squatting as they held up their long wool coats. Their heads were covered in colorful scarves, and they fought for traction on a sheet of yellow ice. They seemed to notice my pause, chuckled with their gold teeth, and began conversing with one another. There was no time to waste, I situated my clothes and my feet onto the small urine glacier. I had found my first opportunity to bond with the people. This was my first "cultural" moment, forever to be etched in my memory bank. It wasn't exactly what I had imagined for my initial point of entry with Central Asian locals, but it certainly grounded me to my new home.

It turns out that the interruptions in our journey to the East were only the beginning of so many lessons learned and relearned. God wants to develop our trust in Him. He wants us to loosen our grip on our plans and ideas. It only makes sense that He must at times interrupt our agendas. Maybe I should let the interruption signal the beginning of the real lesson God intends.

For the days and months that followed, I was humbled by the fact that I got so rattled by a flight connection gone wrong. As the Chechen conflict raged in southern Russia, and women saw their sons dragged behind tanks through the street, who was I to complain about my lack of order and comfort?

Yet, surprisingly, my small life, my little context, and all the minutia I encountered seemed to be on God's mind as well. They were significant

19

and acted as teachers when I let them. My world and my growth were valid no matter how slick or bumpy the path became. The flight that launched us into our new reality set the tone for the next 20-plus years of our lives. So, I often found myself repeating Prov 19:21 like a mantra...

"The plans of man are many, but the Lord's purpose will prevail"
Proverbs 19:21

REFLECTION

1. What is your usual response when plans don't turn out the way you like?

2. What do you think gave Paul the ability to be content with any circumstance? (Phil 4:12)

3. What attitudes and behaviors would someone exhibit who was able to reconcile...
- "making the most of every opportunity" (Eph 5:16) and "be still and know that I am God" (Ps 46:10)?

GOD'S CALLING FOR DUMMIES

Day 3 – by Dan

> "Therefore my brothers and sisters, make every effort to confirm
> your calling and election. For if you do these things, you will
> never stumble."
> 2 Peter 1:10

When pastors and conference organizers find themselves in a bind, I receive phone calls to speak at Christian venues, usually about "whatever is on your heart." More often than not, what is on my heart is something related to God's work in the Muslim world or something He's teaching me through my experiences as a minister. Almost without exception after I speak, a young, bright-eyed, twenty-something will approach me and ask, "How do I know what God wants me to do with my life?" As this question has arisen again and again throughout years of speaking engagements, I realized that people like me wanted a simple step by step formula to discern God's "call." Although God tends to interact with individuals in individual ways, I chose to bypass conventional wisdom and come up with a one-size-fits-all method for the generic way God tends to reveal His calling in peoples' lives:

Step One: Do what God has already made clear in His Word

As I read through Paul's letters in the New Testament, I'm amazed at how confident Paul is in his calling.
"Called as an apostle and set apart for the gospel."(Rom 1:1)
"Called as an apostle of Christ Jesus by the will of God..."(1 Cor 1:1)
Unwavering, bold, unapologetic in his clarity. Yet, nowhere in scripture does Paul mention filling out his spiritual gift inventory, nor completing a Myers-Briggs assessment, nor getting online to discover his StrengthFinders profile. Instead, Paul had a different strategy to determine his calling -- a dynamic relationship of listening and full surrender to the

Father. Os Guinness summarizes this strategy as follows: "God leads forward as we respond to his call. Following His call, we become what we are constituted to be by creation."[iii] The essence of God's calling is to give everything to His service. Calling is revealed through obedience and is not static, but ever evolving. Are we setting aside time to listen to the Lord? Are we surrendering completely to what He has already asked us to do in His Word and through His Spirit? If not, why would He reveal more?

As a junior in college, I spent a fall weekend at a Christian leadership retreat developing a mission statement for my life. The leader asked us to identify tasks we could accomplish on earth that would not be possible in heaven. After an hour of privacy, I came up with at least two: Live by faith and tell others about Jesus. I also identified a couple of verses that summarized these ideas: Galatians 2:20 and I Peter 2:10. My mission statement was born out of those verses;

"To live by faith in the Son of God and proclaim His excellencies."

As it turns out, God had already made clear what my calling was through his Word a couple of thousand years ago, and I just needed the Holy Spirit to highlight how the scripture related to my specific situation. I'm confident that the hour I spent trying to discern which aspects of God's word he wanted to use to shape my unique path was guided by the Spirit. The only question remaining was, would I obey those scriptures in the days, months, and years to come? Would I have the courage to make life decisions in light of my mission?

In the context of a dynamic relationship of listening to and obeying the Father, the first step to determine one's call is to submit to what God reveals through His Word and Spirit.

Step Two: Try It On

In the summer of 1985, that mission statement and the advice of my Bible study leader began to refine my calling. I applied to spend my summer on a two-month project in Eastern Europe. The goal of this project was to travel behind the then-called "Iron Curtain," meet college students, and discover if they were interested in following Jesus. At the time I knew nothing about Eastern Europe, the Soviet Union, communism, or international travel. Beyond a mental picture of people in gray work clothes lined up outside of gray factories with gray smoke billowing out of gray smokestacks, I was a total blank.

This turned out to be an advantage, because my monochrome musings were way off. I ended up with a team of six other Americans in Dubrovnik, Yugoslavia. It was every color except gray. Dubrovnik is a beige colored 1000-year-old fortress city with walls 30 feet thick and 90 feet high set on the brilliant blue water and white rocky cliffs of the Dalmatian coast. Even back in 1985, besides the pictures of Commander Tito hanging in every household, Dubrovnik felt very non-Iron-Curtain-ish. Students from Yugoslavia and Europe flocked to the gorgeous beaches, clear water, and cheap accommodations.

I spent every day and night of that summer with Duane, my giant 270-pound college-football-playing teammate from Amish country Pennsylvania. Duane and I always found a handful of Yugoslavian students to talk with in Dubrovnik's multiple nightclubs and cafes. Each night ended with appointments for the following day to continue dialogue about Jesus and enjoy the coastline of the Adriatic. At the end of eight weeks, we all hated to leave.

Back at Colorado State University, during the academic year, I tried to reach out to students through individual meetings, surveys, campuswide outreaches, and church events. During the course of four years I tried my hand at the multiple forms of work and ministry set before me: public speaking, behind-the-scenes service projects, tutoring math, one-on-one evangelism, leading small group Bible studies, teaching special-needs students, open-air preaching, organizing small conferences, delivering pizzas, debating atheists, and dabbling in international missions. Like trying on shoes at a department store, I wanted to see what fitted best, what felt comfortable to walk in, and what I could see myself wearing for the next season of life.

I've observed throughout the years that God tends to build a calling around our life experiences. The more experiences we take advantage of, the more raw-material God has to construct a blueprint for the future.

Step two in determining God's call is to try on multiple forms of work and ministry to see what fits you best. God has created you with unique interests and gifts, and He will guide you into the activities that resonate with your passions, but it may not be the first (or even the second) venture you try.

<u>**Step Three:**</u> Ask God for Something Supernatural

It was early June, 1986. On the Aeroflot flight from Frankfurt to Moscow, the gruff heavy-set stewardess asked Duane (yes, we were together again) in broken English what we wanted to drink. When Duane asked what the options were, the only thing we understood was Lee-Mon-Nad, which sounded a lot like lemonade, so we chose that. She brought out two glasses of amber colored liquid with a foamy head which threatened to spill over the rim. Duane and I sniffed at it, poked at it with a straw, then bet each other a dollar we couldn't drink it to the bottom. Both of us sensed the attack on our manhood, so in unison we downed the frothy ale. It definitely wasn't lemonade. The grog was followed by a compartmentalized metal tray full of soggy food items I was sure I didn't want to eat, even for a dollar. When we landed in Moscow it only got worse. Supermarkets full of canned seaweed, anorexic chickens, and lines for bread.

Negative feelings of Moscow were accentuated by minimal progress in evangelism and discipleship. Not only did we have zero Russian language ability, but we were constantly followed by the KGB. Any conversation we started with potential English speakers was soon interrupted by a polite well intentioned man in a gray suit who started asking where we were from and why we were interested in talking to Russians.

I was overjoyed to set foot back on American soil, and vowed internally (because it wouldn't sound spiritual to say it out loud) that the Soviet Union was off my list of future travel. Then the thing we all dread happened. God interfered. I woke up one morning in the house I rented with five other college friends. My eyes fixated on the bookshelf across the room lined with at least 100 Christian titles. Almost audibly, I heard God say, "Look at all the resources I given you to grow in your faith. I've also just shown you a place where people have almost no resources and no opportunities to know Me. How can you say you'll never go back?"

From that morning on, I wrestled with the idea of returning to the Soviet Union. But, I wanted some supernatural sign. Like Gideon who waited for God to give a couple of confirmations before moving forward, I asked God for some undeniable epiphany that this was, indeed, His leading.

A couple of months later I attended a large student conference. As a small aspect of the larger program, some mission leaders conducted a breakout session one evening for students interested in serving in Russia. Out of obligation, I attended the meeting and threw up a quick prayer for a supernatural tractor beam to illuminate God's call on my life. With minimal expectation I sat in the back row next to the door. A woman named Debbie addressed the crowd of 100. Half way through her presentation, she stopped as if she just remembered a forgotten agenda item. "Is there anyone here named Dan Krull?" she asked. I timidly raised my hand in confusion. "Come on up here," Debbie continued. "Alex, whom you talked to about Jesus last summer in Moscow, is now following the Lord, and he gave us this box to pass on to you." I jostled my way to the front, gratefully took the box, and started to head back to my seat. "No, open it here in front of everyone," Debbie requested. I tore open the cardboard and pulled out a full Russian military uniform, which was debatably the coolest thing on the planet back in 1986. The crowd cheered. Debbie cheered. And I knew this was all I needed. Thirty years later, I pinpoint this moment as the undeniable pillar of God's specific call for me to serve him in the former Soviet Union until He clearly leads elsewhere.

I also believe that most, if not all, of us need such a supernatural experience. When difficulty and doubt plague us, we need a clear mile-marker to look back on and say, "Remember when God did that? I know without a doubt that this is where I'm supposed to be and doing what I'm supposed to do."

Step three is to dare to ask God for a supernatural sign, and expect that He will provide one.

Step Four: Move Forward

Acts 16:6-7 recounts the travels of Paul and his companions through modern day Turkey. They intended to go into Asia, then into Bithynia, but on both accounts the "Spirit of Jesus would not allow them to." What I find interesting is the backdrop: Paul's team was moving. It was going places. The men weren't sitting around a table back in Antioch waiting for God to reveal every step of the journey before launching out. Because they were moving, God's Spirit could guide them in the right direction. As Bill Bright used to say, "You can't steer a parked car."
Once God has called you in a general direction, through His Word, through your experiences, and possibly through a supernatural moment, move out. You may not have all the details figured out, but as you move forward, His Spirit will do the fine tuning.

"Therefore my brothers and sisters, make every effort to confirm
your calling and election. For if you do these things, you will
never stumble." 2 Peter 1:10

REFLECTION

1. From God's word, what are some principles you believe should govern all our lives?

2. Is there any new direction, activity, or step of obedience you believe God is leading you toward?

3. What would God have to do to prove that new direction was, indeed, His will for you? Ask Him for it.

STAR GIRL
Day 4 – by Dina

> "For He has rescued us from the dominion of darkness and
> brought us into the kingdom of the Son He loves, in whom we
> have redemption, the forgiveness of sins."
> Colossians 1:13-14

The Lenin's Museum of Art on Sovietskaya Street in Bishkek, Kyrgyzstan was an unimpressive concrete building that sprawled unattractively over more gray, concrete ground. But it was a convenient location, with an obvious entry and a theatre style room off to the right, which we could rent hassle free. The theatre was dark, lined with red fabric cinema chairs from wall to wall, minus a narrow passageway on each side. The front consisted of an uneven stage about three feet high.

Each Thursday, English students, acquaintances, and passers-by gathered in this venue for our "New Life" meeting. The meeting aimed to provide a fun atmosphere for college students to meet others, play some games, and explore the topic of Christianity. My first week in-country I was introduced to the 80 students who had come to join the fun. A short-term team had faithfully gathered these students during the months prior to our arrival. We merely capitalized on their momentum and hoped to influence these young minds with life-giving truths.

One such Thursday afternoon, I saw a young lady I hadn't noticed before. She stood out as particularly exotic with her puffy head of dark curls bulging out of her artisan wool cap. Her lips were shining red from across the dim room. Her eyes were lined heavily against a smooth pale face like a china doll in fur! By now, my one line of Russian had developed into many and I managed to have a broken conversation with our new visitor, Jildiz. Jildiz means star in the Kyrgyz language. She was older than the students and a bit more dignified in her approach. No sloppy kisses like the college-aged girls exchanged with each other, but rather an internationally approved handshake and smile. I was relieved that she spoke a fair amount of English. If left to my Russian skills at the time, our relationship would have been limited to age, address, favorite foods and colors. I was intrigued with Jildiz. She offered to spend time together and I eagerly accepted.

Jildiz joined us for dinner at our apartment, which was located on the main street that split the capital of Bishkek down the middle. I had prepared a beef pot pie for our guest. Winter months demanded that Betty Crocker and I get acquainted with the potato, onion and carrot sections of her text. The beef had been recently chopped off a large carcass on a tree stump across the street by the meat vendor and was guaranteed fresh. I had poked it with a stick a few times and decided to believe the meat guy.

After dinner, Dan was eager to leave us two girls alone. He was tired of making conversation all day, and Jildiz's energy seemed to drain the blood out of his face. I, however, was just getting comfortable. Dan gathered our plates and, before I knew it, he was in the kitchen clanking away. Jildiz, wide-eyed and mouth gaping, stared at me as though we were being robbed.

"What's the matter?" I asked.

"What is wrong with Dan? Is he mad?" she lowered her head and whispered.

"Why do you say that?" I replied.

She continued to whisper even quieter, "I hear dishes. He is in the kitchen. What is he doing?"

"I cook, he cleans," I said with a chuckle.

A silence fell on the table between us, and in a more hushed whisper than the last, she stared into my eyes intently with her deep brown, heavily lined gaze, "You are a princess."

I broke the silence with a loud American laugh. "A lot of people do that," I explained. But my explanation wasn't enough for her. She was trapped in her own mind, translating what she had just seen.

Two weeks later Jildiz came back to our home saying she had to speak with me.

"I have been to the village for some time and want to let you know what I told my family," Jildiz started.

Of course, I wanted to hear. I encouraged her to go on, oblivious to the topic of discussion.

"I told them that I have seen true love," Jildiz continued. "Yes, I told them that I saw, for the first time, true love. My grandmother still doesn't believe what Dan did. But I told her it is true, that I saw it with my own eyes."

"Jildiz, what did Dan do?" I asked eagerly, wanting to know myself.

"You are a princess. He treats you as a princess. He loves you. He cares for you. He will never leave you. He is a good man...he cleaned your dishes!"

"Oh, Jildiz! He does love me," I said slightly disappointed. I secretly wished Dan had done a heroic, spectacular deed to prove that our God was real.

"Yes, and the family wants to know what they need to do. Can you teach us? Can you tell me, so that I can tell them? Can you let us know your secret? I've been wanting to know this for so long," Jildiz pleaded.

As Jildiz and I examined the story of God's divine love, beginning with creation and running through the span of time, we also discussed Jildiz's life in fuller color. Married off at 17 to the youngest son of a neighboring family, Jildiz took up her relegated station in their home as the "nevesta"-- young bride. The bride of the youngest son, in Kyrgyz culture, is obligated to care for the husband's parents. This is a common form of social security set up in one form or another for many cultures. After a year of marriage and no pregnancy, Jildiz was sent to a witchdoctor to remove any suspected barriers. A chicken was killed to atone for sins preventing her from carrying a child. The reason for her existence as a woman, even more important than "doing tea," was to bear children for her husband and the legacy of the family line. A boy was an absolute necessity. The family came to resent Jildiz as the days and months rolled by with no baby in sight.

One day when Jildiz was home alone, her father-in-law appeared. He told Jildiz to lie down for him. Jildiz refused, begging this man -- part family, part slave master -- not to betray the sanctity of her marriage. The father forced her to the ground by her hair, screaming that she was ultimately his property, not his son's. That was the day Jildiz was broken, and that was the day she conceived a child.

The walls of the Soviet birthing houses in Kyrgyzstan were lined with metal cots. Expectant mothers provided their own pillows, linens, and towels. Relatives and friends passed food through barred windows. The voluntarily jailed women awaited their moment amidst screams heard echoing through the hallways. Good behavior promoted gentler bedside manner from the staff.

Jildiz gave birth to an 8-pound baby girl, dark haired, rosy cheeked, a porcelain doll. She relived the moment in her mind, eyes glancing out the window, lost in a different time and place. Then she stopped talking, looked down at my carpet below her feet and remained still. I didn't know if I should prod her along in her story, but my better judgment kept me still and quiet with her.

After a heavy silence, she sighed. "And that's all I knew of her."

Anxiously waiting for her to fill in the gaps of the story, I sat edgy on my seat. All I could come up with was, "Why?"

With paralyzed lips and a blank stare, Jildiz concluded, "My husband came to visit. The nurse let him see the baby. When I awoke, I asked why they hadn't brought my daughter to me, like all the other new mothers in the cot-filled room. The nurses kept answering that it wasn't the time. When the doctor finally appeared, the only thing she uttered to me was, 'Your daughter died.' She turned, left the room, and I never saw her again. Days later, when I returned home, I was informed that my husband had taken my child from the hospital. He had discarded my baby in a nearby dump, as a sacrifice for my sins."

Jildiz sadly recounted that following this news, she fled her bridal home and sought refuge with her parents, only to be turned away. She would bring utter shame on the entire household by rejecting her arranged marriage.

Following her escape from her husband, Jildiz had found "refuge" from her hell in the arms of an elderly international man who had come to Kyrgyzstan for the gold industry. Jildiz settled for this life, as it strangely provided her some sense of freedom from her initial oppression, although in actuality, she had merely exchanged one form of bondage for another.

One night at a lake-side resort, Jildiz and her escort were beginning to engage physically when the silver-haired man put his hand to his chest, looked at her with eyes wide-opened and took his last breath. Jildiz laid beneath the lifeless body for a moment, slowly realizing what had just happened. Something needed to change.

With what money she had, she made her way to Kyrgyzstan's capital city and moved into a tiny room with an elderly widow in exchange for cooking and cleaning. Jildiz began to investigate what she could possibly do next; She knew she didn't want to return to either of her former lives. Within her first week in the capital, she found me at Lenin's Museum.

What an odd intersect, what a gracious God. What on earth did I do to deserve the honor of explaining the eternal mysteries to someone in need of transcendent hope? There is no deserving, I was merely available. I went to Lenin's Museum, I met people, I invited them over and hoped for a conversation to turn upward. In the case of Jildiz, I was also blessed with a treasured friend and a redeemed life.

> "For He has rescued us from the dominion of darkness and
> brought us into the kingdom of the Son He loves, in whom we
> have redemption, the forgiveness of sins."
> Colossians 1:13-14

REFLECTION

1. Who are some of the people God has put in your life for this season?

2. In what ways might you reflect Christ's love to them this week?

3. How might you adjust your weekly schedule to be more available to meet the needs of others?

HAPPY TRAILS

Day 5 - by Dan

> "Stop judging by mere appearances,
> but instead judge correctly."
> John 7:24

During one of our first summers of international ministry, our team decided to take a group of 50 students to a popular "lake resort" in the northern part of Kyrgyzstan for a week of Bible instruction, practical training in evangelism, and fun. After a quick budgeting meeting with our team, we agreed to subsidize half the cost of transport and housing through personal fundraising efforts, but require students to contribute the second half--approximately $50. We wanted participants to have some skin in the game and take the project seriously.

Since fifty dollars was an insurmountable goal for many of the students, my wife began a two-month herculean administrative feat of gathering orders for canned goods from the foreign community that lived in our city. She would then distribute orders to students who had been bending gold metal lids onto hot glass jars full of fruits and vegetables since they could walk. Thus, any student who wanted it bad enough could earn his or her $50 and join the project.

July 20th finally came. We loaded film projectors, generators, screens, snacks, and more than the legal capacity of students onto a bus that looked like it had shuttled soldiers to the front lines in the battle of Stalingrad. We set out on our five-hour voyage toward Ak Jol sanatorium. Just the name conjured up images of Arkham Asylum for the Criminally Insane, and upon arrival, the "resort" lived up to its name. Ak Jol, translated 'Happy Trails", was an advertising banner for any movie about "the day after." Constructed in the 1970s for faithful soviet road workers to enjoy their 10 days per year of mandatory vacation, Ak Jol was now a collection of crumbling concrete barracks surrounding a courtyard filled with more broken concrete, protruding rebar, dirt, and weeds. Two open pit toilets, one for men, one for women, serviced the entire sanatorium which housed 250 people. The only consolation was that one hundred yards beyond this little Chernobyl sat the pearl of Kyrgyzstan - Lake Issyk Kul. Almost 200 kilometers long and surrounded by mountains, Issyk Kul is the world's second largest lake by volume of water. Fed by mountain streams and hot springs, swimming in this natural wonder proved refreshingly cool, but not frigid. After navigating weed covered walkways and a gravelly beach riddled with discarded watermelon rinds and corn cobs, closing our eyes and plunging into the water was a refreshing escape from reality.

Rumor had it that Japan considered purchasing lake Issyk Kul in its entirety as a spare getaway for their island nation. However, reconnaissance crews with Geiger counter's reported unsafe radiation levels so they gave up on the dream and let Kyrgyzstan's tourist industry develop at its own pace. That pace hadn't hit its full stride by the time we showed up with our 50 students.

On a comfort scale, Ak Jol was a 2 out of 10. However, as a greenhouse for spiritual growth and faith stretching evangelism, the sanatorium scored a nine. Each morning students gathered for a Bible teaching session. In the afternoons, we organized beach games, skits, and concerts to gather crowds and share the gospel. Most evenings we bounced between sanatoriums showing the Jesus film or putting on performances with a Jesus message. Our students engaged hundreds of Kyrgyz in conversation throughout the week, and confidence levels skyrocketed as students saw God using them to influence others. It felt like we were laying the foundation for the next generation of Kyrgyzstan to take the good news of Jesus' love and forgiveness to their entire nation.

Halfway through the week we had a glitch. A van full of students who had not signed up for the project, nor paid their $50, nor spent the summer canning fruit to earn money, showed up at Ak Jol and joined right in on all the activities. Without any apparent malice, they jumped in the cafeteria line for meals and pulled up a chair at meetings. They volunteered for skits and rolled out their blankets to sleep on the floor with our project students.

How could these students be so shameless in their freeloading off the work and planning of others? What kind of testimony would this be to the management of Ak Jol, now that we were sneaking extra unpaid-for students in through the back door? The lack of honesty was clear. Deception, stealing, sloth, and probably several other of the seven deadly sins were the issues on the table. It was my duty as project leader to set right the wrongs perpetrated by these irresponsible apostates.

The morning after the delinquent students' arrival, I figured it was a good time to teach all the students an object lesson on integrity and honesty. Assuming that everyone would see the pure intentions of my heart, and the obvious behavioral aberrations of the select students, I pointed out their waywardness in front of the entire group. In doing so, I committed the "fundamental attribution error" before I ever knew what the term meant. The "fundamental attribution error" occurs when someone judges himself by his intentions and others by their behavior. It is almost always a recipe for disaster. This instance was no exception.

In the midst of my sanctimonious treatise on integrity, the faces of my young audience began to contort. At a certain point, I became aware that no one was listening to the words coming out of my mouth. The heated looks in my direction and knowing glances toward each other must have been familiar to all pirate captains right before a mutiny. The issue was exacerbated by my complete cluelessness that anyone could have a point of view on the situation other than my own.

Almost immediately there was rebellion in the ranks. Students stopped coming to meetings. Others gave me the silent treatment. Project participants with more daring and maturity tried to pull me aside and help me see the light. It took this jury of 19-year-olds, who had been followers of Jesus for less than a year, to open my eyes to the fact that reality is slightly larger than my limited perception.

The jury's case was pretty strong. They began their attempt to enlighten me by unpacking an opposing point of view:

1) This was Kyrgyzstan, a shame based culture. Rebuking someone in front of their peers was tantamount to murder. Even if the students

34

were in the wrong, there were culturally appropriate ways of letting them know.

2) Central Asia was a communal society where everything is shared. Meals are served on one large plate with everyone grabbing a handful. Homes are shared with four to five generations of relatives. Answers to exams are shared. Salaries are shared. Surely a few paltry cafeteria meals and some floor space was no exception.

3) Wasn't the goal of this project to train students and reach out to others? This van full of late-comers brought more students to train and more manpower to reach out. Maybe they didn't go about it the way I would prefer, but the delinquent students' intentions were to be a part of God's exciting work.

At the time, I heard but didn't listen. I was so convinced of my singular view of events and motives that I failed to apologize. Instead, for the remainder of the week, I struggled to teach through the Sermon on the Mount, met by killing glares and apathetic responses. As I look back from a hopefully more mature perspective, I'm not sure I would change my decision, but I would change how I went about addressing those involved. The verse on judging others is seared in my mind. Judging is not about suspending God's standard of right and wrong, but about listening, seeking to understand, restraining the urge to guess at the other person's intentions, and moving people toward righteousness in a way that honors everyone involved.

Fast forward a couple of decades and I still remember the visceral pain of my "Happy Trails" summer fondly as an invaluable lesson forever imprinted on my path of life.

> "Stop judging by mere appearances,
> but instead judge correctly."
> John 7:24

REFLECTION

1. When are you tempted to judge the intentions of others?

2. What might help you avoid assuming you know other people's motives?

3. When you consider how Jesus deals with you (with patience, forgiveness, commitment to your growth), how can you extend that behavior to others?

GREAT EXPECTATIONS

Day 6 – by Dina

> "For we are God's handiwork, created in Christ Jesus to do good
> works, which God prepared in advance for us to do."
> Ephesians 2:10

I was ecstatic to hear that our first indigenous full-time Christian worker was reporting to our student ministry team in Bishkek, Kyrgyzstan. My Russian language was spotty, but it was enough to get us through a staff meeting. Ainura reported in the fall of 1995. She was a simple, pleasant girl reared in a home that had weathered the rise and fall of the Soviet empire. Her parents were brought up in the mountain villages of Kyrgyzstan, speaking only Kyrgyz. However, when Ainura's parents began rearing their two eldest children, Russian became the language of education in public schools. Therefore, Ainura and her siblings spoke varying levels of Kyrgyz at home and Russian on the street. I appreciated Ainura's capacity to endure my low competency in language. Maybe her multi-lingual upbringing groomed her for such a task.

Ainura's spiritual journey with Jesus had begun a few years prior. Although culturally Muslim, Ainura had wondered about spiritual topics and thought perhaps the Russian Orthodox church would have some answers. She asked God to show Himself to her as she entered the ornately dilapidated onion-domed Orthodox church one sunny afternoon. A Russian "Babushka" pointed her to the candle kiosk where Ainura purchased a long thin candle to place in front of any saint of her choosing. Ainura traversed the dimly lit sanctuary unable to find space left in front of any of the golden icons dedicated to the great fathers of the faith. When the Babushka on duty saw her bewilderment, she pointed to a saint in a far corner. As Ainura reached over the rows of glowing offerings to stick her own candle in the last spot of unclaimed sand, a flame licked the sleeve of her shirt and set it on fire! The quiet room was pierced with Ainura's shriek. The Babushka quenched the blaze with a basin of holy water and a reprimand. Ainura left in disgrace, still searching for God.

Days later, a student approached Ainura while she was sitting on a park bench. She asked Ainura what she thought of God, and if she wanted to know Him personally. Ainura realized that her search was over. God had found her! During the two years that followed, Ainura grew in her faith, attended a year-long ministry training school in Moscow, and returned to Kyrgyzstan as the first full-time minister with our budding organization.

Our first day on campus together was my initiation into the Kyrgyz dorms. Upon entry into the dark crumbling concrete building, we were stopped by a frowning head-scarved grandmother sitting behind a rickety wood-veneer desk. Ainura rattled off some explanation in Kyrgyz to the elderly gatekeeper as we passed by. When I asked what she said, Ainura replied, "I told her we were going to visit."

I asked Ainura if she had friends in that dorm. "No, but we soon will," she said with a smirk. I followed Ainura's lead, but I had an awkward feeling that I was going to be more of a barrier to our time than a help. My fair skin and "yellow" hair made me a spectacle. My language skills were crippled at best. I prayed that God would move in spite of me.

Ainura began knocking on doors. She would simply ask if the student occupants had time to visit and explained that we were with a group called "New Life." The dorm dwellers were rural students reared in Kyrgyz speaking homes, so Russian quickly transitioned into Kyrgyz, leaving me in the dark. To my surprise, not one girl failed to invite us graciously into her room and serve us tea. Each room had a makeshift braided coil of wire jammed into a half-melted electrical outlet which the students used as a hot plate. Kettles were propped up on bricks above the coil to heat tea. If there was no tea to offer, the girls would offer a piece of bread. I mimicked Ainura in everything she did, as to not offend, nor stand out more than needed.

I asked Ainura why these girls let two strangers come into their room with barely any explanation. She replied that the Kyrgyz must let visitors in; they cannot turn them away. Traditionally, an unannounced guest is a sign of God's blessing. Cultural norms paved the way for easy access to these students, but I was conflicted that the rule of hospitality, rather than an authentic desire to listen, dictated our interactions.

As we shared the story of Jesus, most girls admitted that they had heard of Jesus when they studied mythology and religion. For some, Jesus was a fairy tale. For others, an ancient prophet. Most concluded that Jesus was attractive but not someone they could follow. In the Kyrgyz worldview, becoming Christian meant becoming Russian, since Russian orthodoxy was the only non-Muslim religion they were familiar with. The Kyrgyz believed they were born Muslim and would die Muslim. There wasn't a choice in the matter, it was just a part of them, like the blood in their veins.

So, Ainura and I went through the motions, door after door, day after day. I asked Ainura if what we were doing was effective; She replied, "You tell me. You're the American. You've been in ministry longer than I have."

This was ludicrous. Ainura was the insider, the expert if there was one. I barely understood what was being said. With every politely opened door and culturally obligated cup of tea, I became more and more cynical. To make matters worse, it was just a matter of time before we saturated the dormitory with our presence and agenda, leaving no spiritual impact in our wake.

One day things went differently. It started with the usual scowl from the elderly disgruntled grandmother guard, the usual dark smelly halls, and the usual quiet welcome of the first room of students. But then a turn. When Ainura finished sharing the Gospel, I noticed one girl who hadn't asked a single question or made a comment during the presentation. She was lifting her head toward the ceiling and raising her palms upward in the Kyrgyz stance of prayer. This had never happened before--girls didn't pray to invite Jesus into their lives, certainly not on the first visit. Ainura looked at me after the prayer and remarked that the young student had prayed to receive Christ. In disbelief I asked, "Why?" I was fairly certain that it was a congenial prayer, a kind duty, as not to shame her guests with rejection.

We both looked to Asel and awaited her answer. I was certain she hadn't understood a thing Ainura said. Instead, the young student answered, "When you came in my room and I saw that book you are holding, I knew that whatever you said I would believe."

I had come carrying the book *More Than a Carpenter*, by Josh McDowell with the Gospel of John included. The thin book's cover depicted golden sheaves of wheat swaying in the wind. It was the only literature we had printed in the Kyrgyz language.

"When I was seven years old my father died in a car accident. He was a taxi driver in Karakol," Asel began speaking again. "The only thing left in his car was a book he had been reading that looked exactly like the one you have. My mother put it up on a high shelf. It was like a part of my dad's presence in the house. "

"Has anyone read it?" I asked in wonder.

"There is a Muslim tradition of keeping a "holy" book in a high place, to be read only by a spiritual leader. I don't know the reason, but it has laid there untouched for the past 11 years. I know that book cover. I know that title. I've looked at that book all these years as a special part of my father that I never knew. So, that's why I knew that whatever you said must be true." There was no doubt in this young girl's voice about her decision that day, not a quiver of fear. She spoke with resolution and certitude.

Eleven years of wonder about an elusive "holy" book was explained that day. In my faithlessness, I had dutifully toted my little Kyrgyz books that morning, not believing it would make any difference. Yet, more than a decade after the faithful giving of a single book by someone who would never meet me, nor see the fruit of their effort, God worked His plan. What an unexpected mosaic of events, made up of broken shards of pain and wonder. A clandestine distribution project on the edges of civilization, followed by a tragedy, a loss, and now a glimmer of new hope artfully pieced together by our Creator. It wasn't our words, it wasn't our brilliant strategy, it was the missing fragment that the Lord so graciously provided, the colorful piece that brought together a masterpiece of meaning in this young student's life. Ainura and I walked right into a work prepared in advance.

How lowly and insignificant I had felt that day participating as a mere bystander, tenuously connected through intermittent translation. Yet, somehow, time past met with time present and Asel met her Savior. The method seemed lousy, the vessels incompetent -- but God's preparation and design were enough.

> "For we are God's handiwork, created in Christ Jesus to do good works, which God prepared in advance for us to do."
> Ephesians 2:10

REFLECTION

1. When is it difficult for you to believe God has good works already prepared for you?

2. How might you increase your day-to-day awareness that God is preparing your way before you?

3. How does perseverance relate to walking into God's good works?

BUMBLE BEE

Day 7 – by Dina

"A smoldering wick, he won't snuff out, a bruised reed He will not break...,"
Matt 12:20

During those first several years in Kyrgyzstan, I, Dina, spent much of my time with a woman named Jildiz. She became my closest friend. She taught me how to cook Central Asian rice dishes and make curtains. One afternoon she came frantically pounding at our apartment door. I was nervous that once again she was being pursued by a malicious relative. I flung open the door. "What's the matter?" I asked, bolting the lock tightly behind her.

She was holding a newspaper. She spread it on the table, pointing and demanding I read the article of the day. "It's for you. I know it's for you," she nearly yelled. "You are the right people."

We started wading through the Russian newspaper article together. From what I could understand with my limited Russian reading skills, some teenaged girl named Aida had come from a tiny village untouched by modernity to study at the central nursing school in Kyrgyzstan's capital city. Urban life was a shocking contrast to her familiar surroundings of farm animals and head scarves. Cosmetics, contemporary clothes, and cues from Hollywood were the new norm. She met a boy studying at the Islamic institute and quickly gave herself to this young man. After Aida became pregnant, her boyfriend wanted nothing to do with her. Aida turned to an aunt in the city to find support; The aunt advised her to abort the baby before any of her family heard of it.

The distraught Aida decided to end it all by slitting her wrists. She reasoned that if she were to abort an unborn baby, she, herself, did not deserve to live. Her aunt found her in a pool of blood, and an ambulance rushed Aida to the hospital where doctors revived her and aborted the baby.

The article went on to describe how Aida eventually recovered physically. When she did, the boyfriend started showing up at her dorm room again. Aida once again consented to the counterfeit comfort offered and in another few months, she was pregnant again. This time Aida didn't run to her aunt, nor did she consider taking her own life. She viewed this pregnancy as a miracle and prayed, "God, if you exist, please help me. I know I can't take another life. If you're real, show me what to do."

Aida brought her story to the editor of the city's newspaper hoping that a reader might provide food and shelter for her in exchange for adoption rights to her imminent baby. The editor agreed with Aida's proposal and presented her tale of tragedy in black and white.

As we read the final words of Aida's story, Jildiz's eyes bore into mine, "How can this not be for you? You want a baby and you don't have one," she said, as if she was revealing the climax of a mystery novel. "This girl needs to know the love of God -- she's asking for it. Dina, help her, please!"

Jildiz insisted on arranging the appointment with Aida and the editor. Dan and I decided we would attend an interview and see what came of it.

Aida's eyes met ours twice during the 15-minute interview. Short glances, taking in what she could, until she resumed her stare at the floor beneath her feet. Village girls typically were not allowed to carry on conversations with people older than themselves. Dan and I introduced ourselves only to be answered with, "I am Aida."

Later that evening the editor called to say Aida would like to move in immediately, if we would have her. Who was this person? Could her story be trusted? Was this just an impulsive move in response to a heart wrenching story? It didn't seem to matter anymore. She was moving in, and we had decided to ride this thing out until the Lord directed otherwise. We set our minds to preparing a room for Aida. A year earlier we had hoped that this would be our own baby room, but after 12 months of dashed hopes, we started to think differently. Dan and I were confident that the Lord was asking us to receive Aida into our home, even if we got nothing in return.

Aida moved in unceremoniously. She rarely showed emotion, didn't move much, didn't talk much, and definitely didn't inquire about us at all. As the days turned into weeks, I began to invite Aida to every event I attended or hosted. To my surprise, she jumped at the opportunity to join me. Several student Bible studies and discipleship meetings were in our home each week.

This was an unexpected blessing, since we lived on the 5th floor of an apartment building with no elevator. For two months, Aida became a part of my daily activities. The girls in my Bible study gave their testimonies of how Jesus had changed them, breathed hope into their lives, and had met them in their darkest hour. One Thursday night Aida asked how she could experience the same.

I didn't know how much Aida understood, nor how sincere her decision was to follow Jesus, but at times I would look in her room and see her reading the Bible.

"Lord," I cried out, "comfort this girl's heart. Make her into the woman you want her to be. Give her a future and a hope." I felt like I was praying for my own daughter, not because I felt particularly endeared to her personality, but because I realized that without the Lord she had nowhere else to go. She had no one else to trust.

The day came when Aida entered the affectionately named Birthing House #2. Daily, Dan or I would take her food and other necessities. Straining on my tiptoes to reach the metal-barred windows, I would squeeze my plastic bag of apples through to Aida's outstretched hand. Gauze, antiseptic, an array of medicine, bowls of soup and bread all made their way through those rusty bars into Aida's chamber. This daily routine became exhausting, expensive, and ever more inconvenient. I pleaded with God for labor to kick in and a healthy child to come out.

During the two months Aida was in our home, we had appointments at the Kyrgyz White House, hospitals, and the Ministry of Education. Local officials were convinced we wanted to sell the babies organs to make a profit. The US Embassy and local lawyers admitted Kyrgyz adoption laws simply didn't exist. Aida's doctor proposed paying two hundred dollars to have my name put on the birth certificate as the biological mother. The US

Embassy would issue such a child an American passport, but if any documents had been falsified, I would be imprisoned in the United States for fraudulent activity. I was exploring all possibilities. This felt like an Ethics 101 case study in choosing the lesser of two evils.

Sairan ("bumblebee" in Kyrgyz) was born two weeks after Aida entered Birthing House #2. Aida continued to avoid the question we had been asking ever since she moved in, "What will you do with the baby if the government does not allow us to adopt her?" My frustration was growing with Aida as she had never given one thought toward her future with Bumblebee. The healthy baby girl with flushed rosy cheeks, full and round like a plump little bun, had entered the world without a father or a home. We let Aida know well ahead of time that she couldn't return to our home after the birth. So, with the lingering absence of a plan, Dan and I paid for several nights in a hotel room and purchased her a bus ticket back to her hometown. Aida shunned the option of returning home, but as her release day from the hospital drew nearer, she began to reconsider. Daily we visited the hotel room to check on Aida and Bumblebee. The third morning, we found an empty room. The housekeeper informed us that Aida had left that morning. The elderly woman put down her broom and wiped her moist brow with part of the scarf wrapped around her head. With a deep sigh she walked us through her disappointed version of Aida's stay.

"That girl didn't know what she was doing. She went across the street and bought cow's milk at the market. She didn't want to nurse the baby because she was too sore. Everyone knows you don't take milk from a store and give it to a newborn baby! The child was up all night screaming. Our other guests complained. When I came to see the baby, she had broken out in a bumpy red rash all over her body. I don't know what will become of her. The mother and child left this morning in a rush. She said she had a bus to catch."

The disheveled housekeeper went back to her frantic sweeping motion, cleaning out the dusty corners, shaking her head, muttering something under her breath about the ignorant youth of today.

I wondered that morning if we had done the right thing. Was I too selfish, too afraid, too self-protective? Had my grace run out? Had my character run thin? The past couple of months weren't horrible, but Aida's blankness and seemingly indifferent attitude seemed like a jail sentence if we let her take residence with us after the baby was born. Then what would we do? How could we ever ask her to move on once a newborn came home to us? Had I literally killed little Bumblebee?

For the next several years, I wondered if Aida and Bumblebee would ever show up at my doorstep, or if I'd spot her on an overcrowded bus. Would I see her at the bazaar begging for bread? Though the Lord sometimes brings clarity to our stories, there was never a final bow on the package of our encounter with Aida.

The unmet, the undone and the unfinished can be taunting in life, so I choose to believe He is ultimately sovereign over all things. I know that God's still, quiet voice nudged Aida into our home, but I still wonder if it was God who nudged her out into the plan He had for her. Either way He promises...

"A smoldering wick, he won't snuff out, a bruised reed He will not break..."
Matt 12:20

REFLECTION

1. Are there any situations in your life where you don't know if your actions are helping or hurting others? What do you think God is asking of you?

2. When you are uncertain of God's leading, what do you usually do?

3. How might you take a risk to serve someone this week, regardless of the outcome?

DREAM ON

Day 8 – by Dan

> "During the night the mystery was revealed to Daniel in a vision.
> Then Daniel praised the God of heaven"
> Dan 2:19

Sometime in the spring of 1979, the Abundant Life Christian Center down the street from where I lived in western Colorado held an event called "Round Up Sunday." I would have never heard of it, nor attended, had it not been for a new friend named David. David's family had recently come to faith, and through the prompting of David's father and Gene, the youth pastor, David took a risk with me, his new junior-high school friend. He invited me to church. This was the first time that I can remember sitting through an entire church service, which of course was followed by the "Round Up" potluck. I liked David. I liked Gene the youth pastor. And I liked free food, which came to be a regular event due to the hospitality of David's family for the months and years that followed.

Six months after David's family rounded me up, I placed my faith in Christ, finally realizing that either I could pay for my sin, of which I was well aware, or that Christ could pay. I chose Jesus. As I reflect, I also realize that Jesus chose me. No amount of social engineering could have designed all the circumstances that predisposed me to entrust my life to Christ at that time, in that place.

I spent the remainder of my high school Sundays, Wednesdays, and various Saturdays on the receiving end of Pentecostalism. High-volume, energetic traveling speakers, gospel choirs, transformed businessmen, youth rallies, and miraculous testimonies were the norm. If no one was crying or shouting, then something was wrong. Jim from Oklahoma had died in a car accident and after seeing Jesus for a moment returned to finish out his work on earth. Judy was instantly healed from back pain that had tormented her for years. Twice weekly, Roger would stand up in the middle of the service and start saying stuff in another language.

47

Sometimes there was hum-filled murmuring afterward, but sometimes someone would offer up what they understood Roger say. It usually had something to do with the future or a description of some problem someone in the church was having at the moment. I couldn't make sense of everything, but Jesus was real and my friends were real, so I didn't mind the rest.

Following high school graduation, I moved 300 miles away to study engineering at Colorado State University. Zealous to continue in my faith, I filled out contact cards for every student ministry I could find. Each night of the week I attended a different group, silently asking myself if these were the people I wanted as my future friends, and could they help me get to know Jesus better? One such ministry ignited my reason more than my emotions. Group leaders posed arguments for the historical validity of Jesus and the Bible. We explored the disciplines of methodical Christian growth. Not only did they talk about how our faith could influence others, but the next day leaders would take me with them to talk with students in the dorm who had never heard about Jesus. I filled out inductive Bible study charts and memorized entire books of the Bible. We mapped out prayers according to various acronyms and carried those lists of requests around campus with us. I kept track of hours spent sharing the gospel and numbers involved in Bible study. Like the Army commercials on TV, we were doing more before 8:00 a.m. than most people do all day, and becoming all that we could be – for Jesus.

At some point in spiritual boot camp, however, I lost the visceral awe and wonder of the mysterious supernatural. I heard a seminary professor claim that the Christian life is 90% maintenance and 10% magnificence. Maybe he was right. Trusting that God is alive and active even when He's not visibly miraculous is a catalyst for faith and bolsters endurance, but I longed for an expectation that God could and would show up outside of my methods and categories. The summer I decided to enter full-time ministry, He did just that.

I'm not sure what I did that day nor what I ate (which could negatively affect my credibility), but I do remember that night. I went to sleep fretting over the phone calls required to obtain my financial support-raising goals, which our organization required in order to secure full-time employment with them. I laid in bed mapping out my strategy: 90 calls each Sunday night, which would translate into 15 appointments per week. If one out of every three appointments decided to become a financial partner it would take... then I was out, and a vivid dream came in.

I was sitting in a crowded barber shop with a large Asian-looking man giving me a shave with a straight razor. As he swirled his bristly brush full of shaving cream around my neck, he informed me that the razor he was using had special powers. If at any time during the shave the blade slipped in his hands and drew blood, this was a sign that evil spirits were present. I probably should have run for my life at that point, but since dreams are dreams, I just sat there and let him scrape off the lather. As he moved the razor down toward my throat, he suddenly grabbed both ends of the straight blade and shoved the steel through my neck.

I immediately woke in a panic. My subconscious had all the horror it could handle; But even when awake, I was unable to move. It seemed as though a heavy, black spirit like a smothering lead-filled x-ray blanket from the dentist's office was pinning me to my bed and paralyzing my entire body. No matter how hard I struggled, I couldn't move my arms or legs. I lay there motionless, and breathless, wanting it all to stop. My mind couldn't recall any ministry training directed at freeing oneself from the grips of a demon-possessed blanket, so I went Pentecostal. I could hear in my head the words of a long-forgotten traveling preacher, "At the mere mention of the name of Jesus, demons will flee!" So I actually began to sing,

Jesus, Jesus, Jesus
There's just something about that name
Master, Savior, Jesus,
Like the fragrance after the rain

As I began to sing, the black presence left, almost visibly out my bedroom door. Finally free, I tucked back under my covers and kept singing.

Jesus, Jesus, Jesus
Let all heaven and earth proclaim
Kings and kingdoms will all pass away
But there's something about that name[iv]

At some point I must have fallen back to sleep (probably to escape the sound of my own singing).

The next morning I thought about sharing the whole weird experience with some of my well-versed evangelical roommates, but before venturing down that potential path of ridicule, I decided to arm myself with some Bible-based ammunition. Could God speak through dreams to people if he wanted to? A quick study on dreams in the Bible offered up a resounding, "Yes!" More than 20 instances of God speaking to people in dreams surfaced in less than fifteen minutes of searching. Multiple biblical big-hitters such as Jacob and Joseph, Solomon and Daniel, viewed cryptic messages from God in dreams. In one chapter of the New Testament, Jesus' earthly father Joseph was instructed through dreams on five different occasions.

So maybe I wasn't completely crazy. And if I was, at least I was in good company.

Even though I now knew this weird dream could potentially be from God Himself, I still had no idea what it meant, or why an evil spirit would target me. I decided to avoid the awkward conversations with my not-so-Pentecostal friends and simply ponder these things in my heart, as Mary did after her angelic visitation.

One decade later, God graciously shed more light on my dream. I was living in the heart of Central Asia, married with children and knocking on doors in the pitch black, urine-lined dormitory halls of Kyrgyz State University. I'd almost forgotten my distant Asian barber shop blanket interlude. I had more pressing matters to attend to. Kyrgyzstan's college students, who were reared in a stew of Islam, shamanism, and Soviet atheism, expressed interest in exploring the life of Jesus by the hundreds. Our team organized weekly large group meetings, small group Bible studies, and one-on-one appointments to help the next generation of

Central Asia find eternal hope in seemingly hopeless circumstances. Yet, we noticed that several students would intellectually assent to the basics of faith in Christ, but then seem unable to integrate that faith into their daily life.

Almost by accident one young student named Nurlan mentioned that he would like to follow Jesus but that a black spirit would hold him down on his bed at night, almost paralyzing him, and fill his head with doubts. A black spirit smothering people in their bed? Nurlan (and God) had my attention. Without solicitation, several of Nurlan's friends chimed in with similar experiences; Almost every young man in Nurlan's circle described in detail my black-spirit-oppressive-blanket encounter from a decade earlier, minus the Asian barber. I later learned that this paralyzing spiritual visitation was so common that the Kyrgyz and other Turkic peoples refer to nightmares as "Karabasan" or the black press.

When Nurlan and friends discovered that I had battled with the black spirit as well, I instantly had some street-cred with the boys. They were all ears when I suggested a plan to get rid of their nemesis. I figured that none of the shamanistic Kyrgyz knew the words to the "Jesus, Jesus, Jesus" song, so I attempted to share the overall concept with them. "Next time the familiar demon decides to stop by, repeat the name Jesus from your bed and see what happens."

Within a week almost every one of these young men came back rejoicing that the spirits were subject to them, just like the 72 disciples Jesus sent out. Now my task was to help them rejoice that their names were written in the book of life.

Through this experience God reminded me that He is still mysteriously supernatural and refuses to operate on timelines that make sense to my limited perspective. He dabbles in weird topics such as dreams, demons, and barbershops. God is able to orchestrate every experience during the course of our lives to bring about His unseen purposes. What a wonderful (in the literal sense of the word) God we serve.

"During the night the mystery was revealed to Daniel in a vision.
Then Daniel praised the God of heaven" -Dan 2:19

REFLECTION

1. Has God communicated anything to you recently that you thought didn't make sense? If so, what was it?

2. How do you think God might use your current experiences to shape your future?

TALE OF TWO NEIGHBORS
Day 9 – by Dina

"If you really keep the royal law found in Scripture,
'Love your neighbor as yourself,' you are doing right."
James 2:8

Six months after our overseas arrival, we set up residence in a 5th-floor Soviet high-rise by replacing the rotten wood floor, not realizing we were tormenting our unfortunate 4th-floor neighbors by pounding on their ceiling from morning to evening every day for two months. Oblivious to any apartment-dweller etiquette infractions, we settled into our new remodel and went about life as normal. We assumed we were integrating well into Kyrgyz society – talking with other parents in the courtyard, meeting most of our neighbors, and standing in line each morning to purchase milk out of what looked like a petroleum truck. We hosted guests often and even housed Jildiz and Aida for months at a time. However, with each unexpected student that stopped by and every late-hour flush of the toilet, we were unknowingly chipping away at the sweet potential of neighborly love with the owners below us. Nine months later, the neighborly love eroded further when God blessed us with Jack, a baby boy who generated disturbances of his own. Then came the flood...

Dan and I did our shopping most Saturdays at the outdoor bazaar a couple of miles from our house. We would stroll down the heavily populated "Chui Prospect" with our three-month-old baby Jack in tow. The process took a solid four hours as the hole-pocked sidewalks and crowds restricted our pace. When arriving home, we would lug potatoes, onions, cabbage, and a clunky stroller up the five flights of stairs. I was unable to do the lifting on my own, so it required participation of the entire family. This particular Saturday we just reached the top of the stairs when we were accosted by our furious 4th-floor neighbors, who not only cursed our name but promised to involve local police and take us to court.

As a bit of background, the city of Bishkek had an ancient Soviet system of centralized heating that connected a gigantic coal-operated power plant to each apartment in the city via a labyrinth of underground hot-water pipes and eventually wall-mounted radiators. From May through September, the city would shut off all hot-water under the auspices of cleaning the system. Everyone knew it was a tactic for some government officials to pocket a bit of extra money that would otherwise have been wasted on coal. This meant that summers were accompanied by cold showers, cold water for washing dishes, and kids who rarely took baths.

On our fateful Saturday the city decided to refill the dormant hot water system without forewarning. Being on the 5th floor we had small spickets on the end of each radiator to let air out of the system on just such occasions. Little did we know, someone had twisted the faucets open at some point during the summer months, which remained unnoticed while the pipes were empty. On this day, however, with the faucets open, four hours-worth of rusty hot water now buckled our newly installed wood floors and proceeded to cascade into the fourth-floor apartment below.

Since we didn't know exactly how to respond to threats of legal action, and still were clueless that we had already worn thin the nerves of our apartment comrades, we decided to call in a negotiator. Svetlana Petrovna, my Russian teacher, cultural insider, and friend came to my rescue to mediate with the screaming retirees.

As she entered the flooded apartment, Svetlana's stern Soviet approach was blunt and sophisticated. "Where is the damage? Oh, a pillow, that's not so bad. Oh, the ceiling, that's fixable. The floor, doable. There is nothing here that cannot be replaced or remodeled. How much will that cost? I can find a construction brigade to give us a number."

I followed behind in silence, head humbly bowed, glancing at my neighbors but careful not to make direct eye contact.

The accusations started flying. "Do you know how long we have suffered living under these Americans? Do you know how hard it is to have peace in this home? Countless people visit their apartment, stomping feet echoing in our stairwell all day long. For two months they pounded nails into their floor -- our ceiling -- giving us migraines. And the flushing of

54

their toilet at early and late hours. Who lives like this? We can't even sleep. And now they flood the home that we've owned for 50 years!"

Svetlana kept her emotions at bay. "We will fix what is damaged."

"There is no fixing here, we are in distress. We want to sue for psychological damages." my neighbor responded.

Ouch! Not only had I failed to "love my neighbor," but I had failed even to be an upright citizen in this city. Reach the nations with God's love? Shine my light in the darkness? My presence had accomplished the opposite of what I hoped for in answering the call of God to carry the good news to a distant land.

Patching the damaged ceiling took weeks of negotiating. It was difficult because it wasn't about just repairing the apartment, it was about mending a relationship.

One month after the flood I was standing outside my building below the small protruding balconies of each apartment. Jack was sleeping in his stroller while I was broaching the topic of Jesus with Tanya, the single mother on the first floor, who had a bad reputation of having too much "foot traffic" coming and going from her apartment. Out of the sky came a rotten apple which I almost managed to dodge. It glanced off my shoulder. I looked up in wonder. It wasn't apple season, nor did we have an apple tree in our courtyard. There on the 4th floor balcony stood my neighbor with a scowl on her face. Tanya stood in disbelief, also peering skyward. "Did you just see what I saw?" she asked.

How was I to explain what just transpired? God's timing was a bit off. I felt He was leading the conversation with Tanya to a new depth, only to be derailed by my disgruntled neighbor's rotten fruit grenade.

"Love your neighbor as yourself," the scriptures mockingly chanted in my head.

On the bright side, my short explanation of the situation to Tanya solidified to her that I was more than a visitor in her country. Rather, we had settled in, remodeled our old apartment and were rearing our son together with her in this communal setting of concrete block buildings around one patchy square of soil we all shared. She understood the yearly water pipe scenario, the long Saturday trips to the bazaar, and the close quarters that fostered some conflict. There was nothing in my story that didn't resonate in her mind as just another day in the life of Bishkek. What did surprise Tanya, however, was my confession and desire to reconcile with this woman on the balcony.

In December of 1997, my parents visited Bishkek and we decided to take our neighbors a cake for the New Year. I was afraid of this celebratory token backfiring, but my parents nudged us forward. Bringing a gift, with the addition of my parents, would certainly communicate great respect and honor to the average local in Bishkek, but I was still afraid.

We sputtered out a few congenial words as the couple stood speechless in their entry. We gave brief New Year's greetings along with a heavy dose of apologies for the last year's unfortunate events. Then as quickly as manners would allow, we retreated home. I still don't know if our tribute soothed any wounds or was a mere heaping hot coals of kindness on a bitter soul, but we chose to step into the relationship rather than allow offense and passivity to erect a permanent relational wall.

I've found it easy to love my neighbor when "neighbor" means some other person in general, like the people you wave to when walking your dog by their house or the guy behind the cash register at the local market. It seems much harder when the neighbor has a real name and different opinions and doesn't go away when I close my eyes. Maybe this is the love God desires from us. Not a warm, joy-producing sensation, but self-comfort-denying steps to move toward others when everything in me wants to run the other way. That's probably much closer to the kind of love with which God loves us.

> "If you really keep the royal law found in Scripture,
> 'Love your neighbor as yourself,' you are doing right."
> James 2:8

REFLECTION

1. Recall a recent conflict you had with someone. How would you handle it differently next time?

2. Identify a difficult relationship you currently have. What can you do this week to move toward that person?

3. Make a list of five "neighbors" in your life. Take five minutes to pray a blessing on each of those people.

IT COULD BE ME
Day 10 – by Dan

"And pray for us, too, that God may open a door for our
message, so that we may proclaim the mystery of Christ, for
which I am in chains. Pray that I may proclaim it clearly, as I
should. Be wise in the way you act toward outsiders; make the
most of every opportunity. Let your conversation be always full
of grace, seasoned with salt, so that you may know how to
answer everyone."
Col 4:3-6

One Thursday, as I stood on stage in a small dimly lit Kyrgyz theatre struggling to articulate some Bible lesson in Russian, a new student wandered into the door and took a seat in the center of the front row. Wanting to seize the opportunity to make a new friend and share some good news, I made a beeline to his seat as soon as the talk concluded. I discovered that his name was Baish, and that he had mistakenly walked through the door to the auditorium while searching for the men's bathroom. Too embarrassed to leave in the middle of my talk, he suppressed his biological functions and endured thirty minutes of rambling about a topic he had no intention of pursuing.

During the weeks that followed, Baish and I became friends. We spent weekly time drinking tea, sharing our life stories, and discussing the oddities of each other's cultures. One of those oddities was my strange habit of carrying a tattered brown book bag with me around town. Baish would often comment to his friends, "There is my American friend, the one with the bag," and they would all laugh. Baish wondered what was so important that I needed to carry it everywhere I went.

One Friday at tea, Baish asked me if I thought Jesus was coming back soon. Well prepared for just such a question, I pulled a Bible from my omnipresent bag and showed him Matthew 24:14.

"And this gospel of the kingdom will be preached in the whole world as a testimony to all nations, and then the end will come."

I went on to explain that some researchers claim there are approximately 12,000 people groups around the world and that in the first 1900 years following Christ, about 6000 of those people groups had been given the opportunity to hear about Christ through men and women who had taken the gospel to them. Yet, during the past 100 years or so, the gospel had spread to more than 5000 additional nations, which made the remaining task of preaching to all nations well within reach.[v] In short, I didn't know exactly when Jesus was coming back, but if recent history was any indication, his return was right around the corner.

Baish lowered his head and became silent. I took in the solemnness of the moment as long as I could, then asked, "Baish, do you want to ask Jesus into your life so that you're ready when He does come back?"

Baish responded with a silent nod.

"Do you want to ask Him right now?" I continued.

More silence, then his curious reply, "No, I'll do it next Tuesday."

Slightly perplexed, but assuming there was some cultural cue or time management principle I was missing, I politely said "Okay" and asked if we could meet the following Wednesday to see how things went. He nodded again, and we parted ways.

What I didn't realize is that the following Tuesday was Kurban Ait – the Muslim holiday of sacrifice when most self-respecting followers of Mohammed gathered in the central city square of Kyrgyzstan's capitol to hear Muslim clerics recite various versions of Abraham offering his son as a sacrifice. From the periphery, I watched these white-robed teachers with headwear corresponding to their preferred flavor of Islam talk of singing knives and magical sheep. Several thousand men of all ages kneeled and bowed in synchronized choreography. Several thousand men minus one – Baish.

Baish foresaw Tuesday's empty dormitory as an opportunity to bow his knee as well. In the solitude of his vacant room, he poured out tears for the sins he knew he had committed before God and others. He recognized that just as a ram provided substitution for Abraham's son on the altar thousands of years before, now Jesus offered himself as a substitute on the altar of God's wrath. That Tuesday, Baish received the payment Christ had made for his sin and experienced justification, eternal life, and the internal peace of mind that accompanies salvation.

When we met on Wednesday, Baish filled me in on his decision and the need to wait until a moment of solitude before receiving Christ. I congratulated him on the most significant event in his life and expressed my joy in seeing another Kyrgyz brother enter God's kingdom.

"I'm not Kyrgyz," he replied.

"So are you Uzbek?" I asked, knowing that Baish was from the south of Kyrgyzstan along the border of Uzbekistan.

"No, I'm Kapchak," Baish answered with a look indicating I should know what that meant.

Not knowing if a Kapchak was a person, place, or thing, I finally just blurted out, "What is a Kapchak?"

Baish followed with a short history lesson on one of the largest people groups in Central Asia prior to the reign of Genghis Khan. The Kapchaks ruled the fertile valleys of Fergana until the Mongol hordes attacked from the east. Some of the Kapchaks assimilated into the Mongol culture, whereas others were driven all the way to modern day Hungary, refusing to join with Genghis Khan and his warriors. Thus several villages throughout Kyrgyzstan, Kazakhstan, and Uzbekistan were made up of Kapchak peoples with their distinct language, customs and ethnic loyalties.

Then the "what ifs" hit me. What if the unknown Kapchaks were the last people group on earth without a Christ-following member? What if Christ was also waiting from Friday till Tuesday to see a representative from the Kapchaks enter into His eternal kingdom? What if Jesus was rallying the angels that weekend for His triumphant return, because on Tuesday, Baish would be the fulfilment of Matthew 24:14? What if I had a key role in completing God's plan for all nations throughout all of history? What if people wandering around heaven were to point to me and say, "There's the guy who made the game-winning shot for us and ushered in the glorious return of our King." What if?

Well, if you're reading this, then Jesus probably hasn't returned yet. Which is a good news/bad news situation.

The bad news first: Jesus hasn't returned so you and I must press on, not growing weary in doing good for we will reap a harvest if we do not give up (Gal 6:9). Jesus is committed to seeing at least a representative from every nation take his or her place in heaven before he returns. We who are serious about following Christ must therefore arrange our lives to some degree around this same task that lies so close to the heart of God. Whether it's by giving, going, or praying, the task of getting the gospel to all nations is central to the Bible message and invites participation from all of us.

The good news: Jesus hasn't returned, so you and I have the opportunity to be game changers in the greatest task ever given to mankind. You could be the player who makes the game-winning shot. With new opportunities arising everyday through travel, global migration, international students, refugees, social media and satellite broadcasting, the fulfillment of Matthew 24:14 is inches away. You or I may be God's chosen vessel to stumble into a divine appointment of historic proportions. So, let's follow the advice of the apostle Paul, who reiterates our manifold participation in seeing God's purposes fulfilled:

"And pray for us, too, that God may open a door for our message, so that we may proclaim the mystery of Christ, for which I am in chains. Pray that I may proclaim it clearly, as I should. Be wise in the way you act toward outsiders; make the most of every opportunity. Let your conversation be always full of grace, seasoned with salt, so that you may know how to answer everyone." (Col 4:3-6)

REFLECTION

1. Although God wants to use us locally, He has also called us to make disciples of all nations. What do you think your role is in God's global plan?

2. How might you take a step of faith in stewarding your time, treasure, or talent to make disciples of all nations?

3. Who might you partner with in getting the good news of Jesus to those who have never heard?

BARNYARD EQ

Day 11 – by Dan

> "Care for the flock that God has entrusted to you. Watch over it willingly,
> not grudgingly—not for what you will get out of it, but because you are
> eager to serve God. Don't lord it over the people assigned to your care,
> but lead them by your own good example."
> I Peter 5:2-3

Daniel Goleman, the guru of emotional intelligence, notes that scientists describe the emotional centers of human brains as open-loop systems. This means that people rely on connections with other people for their own emotional stability. If I start laughing, other people around me are more likely to laugh as well, even if they don't know what I'm laughing at. Conversely, if I enter a room frustrated and grumpy, my negativity will be felt in tangible ways by others. One person's emotions affect everyone else's. It happens in families, classrooms, offices, and on football fields.

According to Goleman, the emotions of the formal or informal leader of any group are more contagious than the emotions of others. In the vast majority of situations, everyone watches the leader. [vi] Leaders, whether they are CEOs, or moms, or shift managers at McDonalds, enter the room optimistic or in a funk. They give praise or withhold it, criticize well or destructively, offer support or turn a blind eye to people's needs. They can give meaning to each person's contribution – or not.

It was no mistake that Jesus referred to leaders as shepherds and servants. They have the power to put entire groups of followers at ease by figuratively leading them beside still waters by exemplifying calm confident emotions of their own. Leaders bolster confidence, feed truth and encouragement, and put fears to rest through optimism and enticing visions of the future. They also have the potential to lord it over others and crush souls in their wake when they give in to anger, frustration, and negativity.

In the small village of Tash Konak, outside the city of Bishkek, Kyrgyzstan, lived a five-foot-tall, bright-eyed, 60 year-old grandmother named Danagul Eje. She embodied much of what Goleman and Jesus claimed to be true of leaders. Danagul was the matriarch of her own tribe of three daughters and seven grandchildren, who all lived in her cozy mud-brick home surrounded by sheep, a cow, several turkeys, and a tractor. Delinquent husbands of Danagul's three daughters came and went, but the ten blood relatives were Danagul's true clan. Danagul had been a tractor mechanic during Soviet times so her hands were creased with permanent black lines of engine oil and diesel fuel. She also had the grip of a ultimate fighting contender, which probably explained why the dread-locked grandkids snapped to attention when she spoke. Since the Soviet Union collapsed a few years earlier, Danagul tended farm animals to support her household, and she moonlighted as the village equipment repair expert when jobs arose.

We met Danagul through a mutual friend who had started a home church in her village. Danagul had come to faith in Jesus a few years before we met and had begun the long process of leading her relatives to the Lord, as well as standing up against the social shunning by other families in her Muslim village. Because the village now identified her as a Christian, her work opportunities diminished. Neighbors refused to offer her the jobs they previously sent her way, and her already difficult life in rural Central Asia became even more challenging.

Sometime around our son Jack's first birthday, our family visited the Danagul estate to share some humanitarian aid and see if we could spur on their journey as new believers in Jesus. Upon entering the courtyard, dogs began to bark, turkeys and sheep scattered, and a symphony of barnyard noises gave empirical backing to that Old MacDonald song.

In typical Kyrgyz fashion, Danagul shared every bit of food she could gather and stoked the furnace on the cool fall afternoon so that we foreigners would be comfortable. During our conversation, she described the management of her farm. In order to provide for her daughters and grandkids, at 60 years old, Danagul spent summer nights sleeping outdoors with a rifle in her grip next to her flock of sheep. She needed to ensure their safety from predators and thieves. In the daylight hours, she tended to the unending medical needs of injured or ill grandchildren and ailing farm animals. Yet, she never seemed to complain. She only told the stories to share how the Lord was taking care of her needs and providing for her family. Her permanent smile and calm eyes seemed to shower her household with a sense of contentment.

After several hours of eating, drinking tea, reading some Bible verses, and watching smudge-faced kids unwrap toys and toothbrushes, we navigated the "goodbye – no can't you stay longer" dialogue and mobilized toward the dirt road to hail a taxi home. But as we were exiting the courtyard, Danagul stopped abruptly, announcing that she remembered it was Jack's birthday. She ran back in the house and came out with a roll of cloth under her arm. She straightened up as if to sing the national anthem, then let out a primal gurgling sound which I was unaware humans could make. Immediately, from behind sheds and bushes and holes in fences emerged tens of turkeys answering the call with songs of their own. Danagul gurgled again and the turkeys chattered back. She was Doctor Doolittle in a dress and head scarf. The conversation continued until the gaggle of turkeys (technically a "rafter" of turkeys, according to Google) stood calmly at her feet rubbing up against her like neglected cats. These same animals that had fled from my strange voice earlier were now drawn to the voice of their shepherd (or whatever you call a turkey herder).

At this point, Danagul calmly bent down, grabbed one unfortunate bird by the feet and stuffed him head first into the burlap bag she produced from under her arm. She tied off the bag and proudly handed it to me as Jack's birthday gift. As my mind raced to figure out what to do with my first live turkey in a bag, I smiled, hugged her, and said thanks.

Although she never heard of Daniel Goleman or Emotional Intelligence, Danagul's voice of servant leadership created an emotional loop in her rural kingdom. It brought stability and peace to grandchildren who would otherwise roam the village looking for attention elsewhere. Though she was only beginning her journey of discovering the teachings of Jesus, she exemplified I Peter 5:2-3 by leading her daughters into biblical truth and guiding them to fountains of living water. And maybe, most impressive of all, she even spoke with animals who knew their master's voice and obeyed.

Probably without intention, and definitely without a college degree in psychology, Danagul had created a bit of Shalom in an otherwise oppressive environment. She had accomplished what CEOs and moms and shift managers strive for – creating order and joy out of chaos, simply by leading as best she knew how; by leading as she understood Jesus wanted her to.

So for all of us who are wondering if stress or serenity will win the day, there is hope. The simplest of us, armed with the words and the example of Christ can infuse our environments with the contagious joy that creates emotional stability for those we shepherd.

> "Care for the flock that God has entrusted to you. Watch over it willingly, not grudgingly—not for what you will get out of it, but because you are eager to serve God. Don't lord it over the people assigned to your care, but lead them by your own good example."
> I Peter 5:2,3

REFLECTION

1. How have you seen your emotions positively or negatively affect those around you?

2. In what spheres do you see yourself as a leader or having influence?

3. If one result of the Spirit-filled life is self-control, how might Jesus help you grow in your emotional intelligence?

MUMFORD AND SONS

Day 12 – by Dan

> "So then, just as you received Christ Jesus as Lord, continue to
> live your lives in him, rooted and built up in him, strengthened
> in the faith as you were taught, and overflowing with
> thankfulness."
> Col 2:6-7

Our son Jack was a year and a half old when the unannounced midnight visitation from Doctor Plaster occurred. As I cautiously cracked open the portal to our slumbering fifth floor apartment in Bishkek, Kyrgyzstan, I was surprised to see an English couple named the Munfords (no relation to the band) flanking Doctor Burt Plaster on each side. After catching their breath from the 50 foot climb up the poorly lit stairwell, the three stepped through the steel security door; all wore unusually somber looks on their faces.

On most days the Munfords provided the expatriate community living in Kyrgyzstan with comic relief. Chris, the husband, was always over-exaggerating some recent foible of running over a neighbor's herd of sheep or a botched home remedy for some unmentionable ailment. Linda, the more rational of the two, could be counted on to refute most of Chris's stories as entirely false or a compilation of half-truths. This didn't seem to deter the stories from getting longer and louder with the telling, until Chris's voice was drowned out in a sea of surrounding laughter and Linda's cries of denunciation.

Burt, on the other hand, was a stable, intelligent, thorough, compassionate, and selfless general practitioner who had moved his family to Bishkek to help reform the disastrous post-soviet medical system--a system that contributed to, rather than abated, the suffering of those subjected to its care.

Earlier that day we had approached Burt Plaster to have him take a look at the ring of swollen red skin around Jack's eye. Burt didn't say much

67

at the time, so we assumed it was just pink eye and went about our business. This evening, however, the good doctor sat us down and explained that he had been pondering Jack's condition all day and had brought the Munfords over as additional prayer support. Furrowed brows replaced smiles and heart rates increased.

"I think Jack may have periorbital cellulitis," stated Burt calmly.

The tone of Burt's voice, combined with the ominous sound of whatever it was he had just said, produced added discomfort. Dina's fingernails bore into my forearm.

"Periorbital cellulitis is an infection around the eye that I'm afraid may have gone behind his eye as well. This could possibly spread to the brain and cause meningitis," Burt continued.

Scenes of our toddler in one of those bendy hospital beds, surrounded by blinking blue metal boxes, mummified in a head bandage and connected to clear plastic tubing immediately flooded our parental imaginations. We snapped back to reality when Doctor Burt advised, "So in addition to starting him on some strong antibiotics, I'd like to give him a spinal tap to make sure there is no infection in his spinal fluid."

At some point shortly thereafter, Burt extracted a very grown-up sized needle out of his bag, which he had spent the entire day running from hospital to hospital to find, and asked if I thought I could hold Jack tight enough to make sure he didn't move during the procedure.

Hoisting Jack up onto the kitchen table, I positioned one elbow around the back of Jack's knees and the other around the back of his tiny neck. Under guidance of the trusted doctor, I slowly squeezed. Jack folded and molded into a rainbow-shaped arc. I sought the balance between steady and smashed. My face buried into his tiny smooth temple as I attempted to whisper words of reassurance amidst the whimpering. Even though I had to look away as Dr. Plaster's steady hand inserted the needle, I could tell what was happening by the quivers, flinches, and tightening of Jack's body. What seemed like an eternity later, lab tests revealed that no infection had spread, and the antibiotics effectively eradicated the remaining eye infection.

Almost two decades after this incident, I read Colossians 2:6,7 which commands us to live our lives in Christ...overflowing with thankfulness.

When God decided to answer the prayers of the Munfords through the skilled hands of Burt Plaster, or when He saw fit to deliver us from financial ruin on multiple occasions, or when a friend grabbed one of my kid's arms to keep him from plunging into the frothy torrent of a mountain river, thankfulness overflowed from a fountain within me that didn't need any priming. I wasn't obeying a command, but involuntarily expressing the flood of gratitude that naturally saturated the moment.

I do need a bit more prodding from God's word to overflow with gratitude for the little things; for a body able to ride a bike, for a wife who daily creates culinary masterpieces, for a job that invites creativity and meaningful relationships, for indoor plumbing, and a neighbor who brings me peaches. I need to peer purposefully into the history of God's wonders, and by reviewing the laundry list of His mercies, refuel my heart to live in the joy of gratitude. My tendency is to forget. My default is to dwell on the cost of groceries that my healthy teenage son consumes, instead of the God-sustained health of that same grocery-consuming son. In between crises and undeniable answers to prayer, I need to overflow with gratitude out of choice, because gratitude is the only appropriate response when reviewing the bigger picture of God's marvelous work in our lives.

The follow up question now arises – "Why would God so value thankfulness?" In my limited moments of meditation, I've concluded that gratitude transforms my soul to acknowledge the truth of God's sovereignty. By soul I mean my intellect, emotions, and will. When I am grateful, my mind is forced to admit that God is good and He is in control, instead of insisting on the false notion that the universe exists to serve my fickle desires. In gratitude, my emotions rise from fear, frustration, and anger to peace and a hope that He has an invisible perfect plan. When I'm thankful, my will chooses to honor divinely revealed truth and contemplate a way forward instead of attacking those whom I perceive perpetrated the most recent personal injustice. Gratitude, like all God's other commands, turns out to be for my own benefit.

I also recognize that gratitude may require greater faith for those who didn't receive the positive medical report, or didn't escape financial ruin, and who didn't have a friend close by to save their child. Last March during an outreach concert, an angry drunk attacked one of our Central Asian musicians in a stairwell and took his life. Aziz was our ministry's team leader overseeing the event. After the horror of walking in on the murder scene, Aziz spent the next several months at the offices of the secret police answering loaded questions and refusing to pay large sums of money to make the whole ordeal go away. Once the stress-induced headaches began, Aziz's wife Nilufer pleaded with him to make a change. Aziz resigned his leadership position and moved his family back to their home village for a time of restoration. Three months later, the headaches remained, along with kidney, liver, and back problems.

Nevertheless in the midst of their distress, Aziz and Nilufer refused to complain, refused to quit investing their lives in others, and chose to overflow with thankfulness. I often wonder where they found the faith to do so. Then I'm reminded that in their remote, Islam-saturated surroundings, out of necessity or discipline, they chose to live out Colossians 2:6-7. There was nowhere else to go. There were no TV series to numb their pain, nor shopping, nor travel, nor kids' sporting events to refocus their attention. Jesus was real, and He was ever present to them. They simply continued to live their lives in Him, daily operating out of the faith they were taught. And the result was overflowing gratitude.

So, the instantaneous gratitude of the Munford's answered prayer and the disciplined gratitude of Aziz pressing through hardship are expressions of the same truth -- God is in control. Thankfulness aligns our hearts with that truth and brings us into satisfying harmony with the sovereignty of a loving heavenly Father.

"So then, just as you received Christ Jesus as Lord, continue to live your lives in him, rooted and built up in him, strengthened in the faith as you were taught, and overflowing with thankfulness."
Col 2:6,7

REFLECTION

1. What are some things you are readily grateful for?

2. What are some setbacks in your life that are difficult to be grateful for?

3. Besides the fulfillment of obeying God's command, what would be the practical benefits of greater gratitude?

THE BOXER

Day 13 – by Dan

> "Above all, love each other deeply,
> because love covers over a multitude of sins."
> 1 Peter 4:8

Shortly after arriving in Central Asia in 1995, my wife and I became acquainted with a gold-toothed, smiley, formerly Muslim student named Max, who chose to commit his life to following Christ. Max was from the Kyrgyz mountain village of Kara Kulja, population 11,750, where he knew of no believers other than himself. Whether out of a prompting from God, or naïve adventurism, our Kyrgyzstan-based team and a partnering church from the USA determined that Kara Kulja was going to hear the good news of Jesus' love for them.

In the spring of 1996, six businessmen from this partner church arrived in Bishkek, the capital city of Kyrgyzstan. They were armed with huge hearts, southern drawls, and a Jesus-film projector. After four hours of sleep, my wife and I fed them a light breakfast, and an even lighter portion of cultural do's and don'ts. We then introduced the team to local translators and sent them on a "rustic," yet functioning, Soviet prop plane over a 15,000-foot mountain range. From there the six brave souls endured a three-hour bus ride to their target audience in Kara Kulja. Before leaving, one of the American team members joked, "We're gonna wear this film out in that village!"

Two days later, the bewildered team called from a hotel sixty miles from their intended destination, wondering what to do with the remainder of their week in country. As it turned out, only minutes into the first showing of the Jesus film in Kara Kulja's tattered school building, village elders interrupted the show and asked everyone to leave. They politely instructed the Americans to turn off their generator, roll up their extension cords (since the school had no electric outlets) and find a ride out of town. The elders weren't necessarily opposed to the film's content, but they were offended at not being consulted for permission, nor invited to the premiere showing. We gathered our southern friends back into various forms of transport and convinced them that such setbacks were par for the course.

The pep talk must have worked because the same church rallied around a new vision for 1997. Together with a medical humanitarian aid organization, we plotted together to refurbish a dilapidated medical clinic in Kara Kulja. By doing so, we hoped to pave the way for future teams to take in the gospel. Enough medical equipment was donated to fill a 40-foot container, and our partnering church raised ten thousand dollars to pay for the shipping. When the container arrived in country, an expatriate missionary-doctor with several years' experience in Kyrgyzstan accompanied the cargo to its destination. His job was to present the equipment to the proper authorities and explain its usage to the clinic's local staff.

Three months after original delivery, a teammate and I traveled back to the remote outpost to see how the clinic was progressing. Upon arrival, we were met by the clinic's startled director who wondered why we had come, and if we could pay for his lunch. After we shelled out the $3 to cover his meal and explained our intentions, he slowly put on his coat and walked us from the cafe to the main medical building. Ten steps from the door, a beaming 40-year-old woman in lab coat and head scarf ran toward us with her arms extended wide. She grabbed us by the hand and pulled us to a field behind the main building where she was growing medicinal herbs in a small fenced-off garden. Also gold-toothed and smiley, she explained how some pieces of the equipment we had sent were great for storing the herbs she was growing, and asked if we had any ailments which some combination of her flora were sure to cure.

The director then escorted us back inside where he opened a closet storing all the donated equipment. Since the hospital administration didn't want to pay the electric bill to plug in these modern appliances, like heart rate monitors and EKGs, clinic personnel had neatly piled the western technology behind closed doors. The director proceeded to discourage us from feeling the need to return, but if we did, could we bring him some real Indian tea from the big city?

At this point, some type of red flashing light went off in my mind questioning the effectiveness of our well-intentioned strategies. Maybe I should go back and dust off those old manuals on cross-cultural understanding and asset-based community development, or whatever it was called. That sounded like a lot of work, so instead, I figured we just needed a bigger and better strategy to get to the heart of the Kyrgyz.

That bigger and better strategy came in the form of a world champion welter-weight kickboxer named Aaron. Kickboxing is arguably the most popular sport in Kyrgyzstan, and in 1998, the country boasted reigning world champions in several weight categories. So it was obviously a sign from the Lord that the very same church that we had so effectively mentored in the film and medical arenas, now just happened to have a former world champion kickboxer named Aaron in its congregation. Not only that, Aaron was willing to help us create the queen- mother of all Spirit-inspired outreaches to the Kyrgyz. The plan involved coordinating with the Kyrgyz Kickboxing Federation to host an exhibition match between Aaron and one of their champions. Then, when the stadium was packed with wide-eyed fight fans, Aaron could share how Jesus had changed his life and invite others to follow suit.

The Kickboxing Federation took one look at the plan and politely said, "No, thanks." The president of the federation, who was articulate and gracious, explained that Aaron was world champion six years earlier, and in kickboxer years, that's like 100. The Federation was afraid that any one of their young guys would hurt or kill Aaron, then where would we all be?

Discouraged, and somewhat intimidated by the room full of sweatsuit-wearing combatants, I rose to the leave the meeting. Just then, some visionary from the other side of the large conference table suggested a better plan -- turn the event into a youth bout with 10 junior matches and only one round of exhibition at half time? That way, Aaron had less chance of dying and the exhibition would be a small part, instead of the entirety, of the event. Everyone seemed pleased with the idea. We smiled and agreed and confirmed that Aaron would have a few minutes of talk time to inspire the youth. This, of course, was yet another confirmation that God was smiling on our bigger, better, albeit violent, brainchild.

When Aaron arrived, he looked the part of a fighter. Underneath a thin layer of skin, his head looked a bit like a tin can that had been kicked around the alley for a while by a pack of unruly kids. Not that he looked bad, he just looked well-worn. It all made sense when he told the story of his world championship bout six years prior. In round three, a kick to his face sent his jawbone back through his inner ear, which adversely affected his balance. Yet, by sheer determination, Aaron fought through the next eight rounds until he landed a kick that broke his opponent's arm and won him the fight. All this gave me slightly more confidence that Aaron probably wouldn't get killed before talking to the crowd about Jesus; at least not without putting on a good show.

Match day arrived, and thousands of spectators filled the central stadium just as we hoped. Children in matching athletic warm-ups, aged six to twelve, stood in orderly lines on each side of the boxing ring, one team in red, the other in white. The announcer introduced the youth, Aaron, and Ulan his opponent. Then one of our brothers from the USA sang a flawless rendition of America's national anthem to kick off the first match (pun intended).

It was at this point that the bright shiny sunbeam of Jesus' love for the Kyrgyz became a bit cloudy. I watched one pair of young boys after another punch and kick each other until one started bleeding, or crying, or both. The crowd would throw insults at the loser, and cheer on the winner to keep fighting, even when blood stained the mat. That flashing red light started going off in my head again. This time it was accompanied by neon words: "What are you thinking?"

When Aaron and Ulan launched their exhibition, things got worse. Calls rang out from the audience, "Kill him!" "Why are you faking it?! Hit him!" The longer they fought, the louder the jeers. In light of this less-than-positive vibe in the arena, the half-time gospel speech didn't have quite the effect we were hoping. The thousands of comment cards we expected from spiritually thirsty kickboxing fans never materialized.

On the bright side, Aaron made it back to the US alive and upright. I was also cured of believing I could engineer God's kingdom expansion through bigger, brighter events, or the infusion of lots of material resources.

So, how did the number of Christ followers in Kyrgyzstan grow from 400 to 25,000 between 1990 and 2005? It wasn't so much by big events as by little acts of love, hospitality, and service, which tended to override any of the other stupid things we tried.

Charles, one of the members of the partner church, befriended a few Kyrgyz men each time he visited. Several of these men eventually trusted Christ and Charles helped where he could to foster their spiritual growth. What attracted these men to faith was not an event, nor a cure for some ailment, but the evident love and willingness to serve, which Charles and several others demonstrated over time and distance. One fruit of Charles's influence was a Kyrgyz man named Reza, who currently leads a church planting team in northern Kyrgyzstan. Reza's team now travels from village to village sharing Christ's love and sees hundreds of hopeless families find new hope in a personal relationship with God.

I fear that God may still hold me accountable for all the foibles I've choreographed during my dubious missions career, yet I hold fast to the promise in 1 Peter 4:8-10. Love, hospitality, and service to others may, indeed, overshadow all the ridiculous escapades I've devised and eventually make Jesus look good to all the nations.

"Above all, love each other deeply,
because love covers over a multitude of sins."
1 Peter 4:8

REFLECTION

1. What are some regrets you have in your relationship with God or others?

2. What would it look like to love others deeply in your current life circumstances?

3. Read back through 1 Peter 4:8-10. It would seem that hospitality and service are connected with loving others. Identify one act of service you would like to show to demonstrate love this week.

FOCUS

Day 14 – by Dan

> "'Wake up, sleeper, rise from the dead, and Christ will shine on
> you.' Be very careful, then, how you live—not as unwise but as
> wise, making the most of every opportunity,
> because the days are evil."
> Eph 5:14b-16

I work for an international Christian organization intent on making disciples of all the nations. From the inception of this ministry back in 1951, the singular focus has been to glorify God by helping to fulfill the great commission in this generation.

So, you would think that singular focus would penetrate all I do. Well, not quite. Several years ago, as the Central Asian winter was slowly retreating, we were living smack dab in the center of a Muslim mission field. Outside our gate we were surrounded by the blatant material needs of homeless and alcoholics who roamed our street. In our home, we encountered the spiritual needs of college students who stopped by daily for counsel. Yet, my mind often wandered to less lofty ambitions, such as buying a bike off the Internet. It was in the midst of such attractive distractions that God orchestrated a phone call that pulled my focus back out of the danger zone.

Alex was on the other end of the phone line late that spring evening. Alex led a team who intended to show the Jesus film to every man, woman, and child in Tajikistan. He was calling to invite me to interview some potential staff candidates. Although I liked Alex and admired his visionary zeal, I formulated all the reasons to reject his offer before he even finished his sentence. Tajikistan was on the backside of a recent civil war; City parks were now devoid of trees, as residents plundered whatever fuel they could to heat their homes. Furthermore, Tajikistan was known to be even stricter in its observance of Islam than other Central Asian republics. Therefore, I doubted that any of Alex's disciples could meet our stringent staff requirements: At least three years of following Christ, completion of four levels of evangelism and discipleship training, and at least three generations of disciples underneath them.

After I had delivered my laundry list of rejections to Alex, he assured me that his candidates met all the criteria, that Tajikistan was safe-enough, and that he would personally meet me at the airport to ease any lingering concerns I might have.

Now I was stuck. Although up for adventure, and somewhat intrigued by a visit to the Taliban's bedroom community, I wasn't wild about investing a week in what I predicted to be a waste of time, energy, and resources. Nevertheless, I packed a small bag, boarded an old Soviet aircraft and careened into the capital of Tajikistan -- Dushanbe. Alex and what appeared to be either bodyguards or large scruffy servants met me at the airport and whisked me away to a mountain retreat center where more than 100 new believers and disciple makers were gathered for a week of training. Entrance into the compound included several layers of barred metal gates, followed by a precarious walk across a raging river on a bridge whose base was made from two spindly, wet, and slippery, pieces of flexing rebar. Once inside, heat was sparse, food rations were sparser, but the joy factor was high. Those gathered for the training viewed this as heaven. To gather with other believers in Jesus and talk freely with like-minded brothers and sisters was a luxury most had never experienced since coming to faith. Later, I was to discover that the meager heat and rations were also a step up for most of the participants who were accustomed to long cold hungry winters in Tajikistan's mountain villages.

The following morning Alex ushered me into a room and introduced me to Vos. Vos looked twenty-something with dark hair, thick brows, tan skin, and eyes like a grade schooler who had been sent to the principal's office, unsure yet trying not to show it. His Russian language was as flawed as mine, but we had no problem understanding each other.

Seeing his level of discomfort, I tried to make small talk by asking him to tell me where he was from. He explained that he had grown up in a village in the Pamir mountain range 100 kilometers from the nearest paved road. Vos came to Dushanbe to attend university, and it was there that a friend first introduced him to Jesus Christ and the story of salvation.

Once Vos began to talk, his nerves seemed to settle, so I launched into the official interview questions, hoping he might surprise me, but still doubting he was staff material.

I read question number one, "How many people have you seen trust Christ with you over the past two years?"

Vos was quick to answer, "Forty-two."

"That's pretty good," I mumbled under my breath, yet assuming either he didn't understand the question, or that the Tajik ministry had put on a concert or some big event where 42 people raised their hand to indicate a decision and then disappeared, never to be seen or heard from again. So I asked question two. "How many of those 42 new believers have you personally worked with to help grow in the Lord and continue on in Bible study?"

Vos looked a bit puzzled by the question, but after a second replied, "Forty-two."

"So where are these 42 now?" I asked, veering from the interview questions to clarify any discrepancies once and for all.

Vos scooched up to the table a little bit, straightened his shoulders and looked me in the eye, now like he was the principal and I was the grade schooler in his office.

"You see, Mr. Dan, our desire is to get the gospel out to the entire nation of Tajikistan, so I divided the 42 disciples into six different teams that are now spread throughout the northern part of the country. Every three weeks, I visit each of the teams to see how they're doing and make sure they are continuing to take the gospel to their designated region of the country."

Now I was feeling like the grade schooler, so I just looked back down at my paper and picked the first question I saw. "How do you plan your time?"

Vos, who had never seen a Day-Timer, much less a Google calendar, confidently walked through his yearly goals, six-month goals, three-month schedule, and then a day-to-day account of activities to accomplish all he hoped to see God do through himself and his teams. Offhandedly, Vos mentioned that he feared missing one day, because that could throw off his travel plan, possibly preventing some villages from getting to hear the gospel. Vos then invited me to accompany him out to one of the villages the following day to see how it all worked and to remove all doubt.

The next morning was filled with other staff interviews. So, shortly after lunch, Vos pulled up to the front of the compound in a white, rusty, Russian made Neva. The Neva was the mini-jeep of choice for most mountain-dwelling former Soviets. It was cheap, had four-wheel-drive that worked on occasion, a short wheelbase for maneuvering through tricky mountain switchbacks, and made to run well for about three days in a row before breaking down. Tajiks, like most Central Asians of this era, had more time than money, so the inconvenience of weekly visits to the repair shop was more than offset by three-dollar repair costs.

Almost immediately, we started driving up. Perched at the top of a dozen or more switchbacks was our first destination, a tiny village of 20 homes. As we pulled into town faces appeared in the doors of almost every home until we stopped in front of a droopy wooden shack with tiny wings of green paint peeling up off of every individual board. A rickety fence bordered the property and descended parallel to what looked like a sledding run from front gate to front door. A thin layer of snow and ice encased what appeared to be stepping stones in fairer weather. As I soaked in the sights and smells, a bent-over elderly woman of equal height and width with a large toothless smile appeared in the doorway and beckoned us inside. Using the fence as a makeshift ladder, I gingerly dug one foot into the snow and the other on a conveniently located fence picket. The picket snapped and I tobogganed on my back, feet first, right into the woman's mud room. As she welcomed me into her home, I wondered how, or if, she ever left this shelter between November and May.

Once Vos repelled into the home, Banu, our hostess, sat us in her living room on the cushions of honor farthest from the kitchen and closest to the non-functioning coal-burning heater. Ten similarly shaped women began filling the room. All the men in the village had fled to Russia seeking employment. Tiny amounts of money trickled back to their families to sustain their sparse existence. The women sitting before me comprised a weekly Bible study that Vos had led for the past year.

Vos began by inquiring how the women were doing. One complaint after another filled the air. One women spoke of kidney failure due to an inability to buy coal to heat her home. Another spoke of arthritis, again due to the cold and lack of a bed. Just then a woman stood with her nine-year-old daughter and asked Vos to look at her daughter's head. Covering the back of the dainty girl's neck and spreading into her hairline was a brownish blackish growth that looked like a giant mole. The mother explained that this "fungus" had started several months prior and kept spreading. The mom had tried to scrape it off with a razor blade, but the fungus returned. Neither homemade remedies, nor medicine from the doctors down in the city seemed to slow the growth. After a brief exchange in the Tajik language that I didn't understand, Vos turned to me and asked if I could lead these women in a Bible study on how to persevere through difficulty.

I quickly scanned my memory banks for anything in my life that could possibly be labeled as suffering. Let's see...I grew up for a time in Hawaii hounded by the daily choice of swimming in the pool or the ocean. From there I moved to a ski area in Colorado where I skied almost daily in the winter and rode motorcycles through postcard-worthy aspen groves in the summer. Privileged to attend a four-year university, then on to a teaching job in Salzburg, Austria – possibly the quaintest city on the planet. Honestly, and pathetically, the only thing that came to mind was the pesky dilemma with the Internet bicycle purchase. Fortunately, I was self-aware enough to realize that sharing my online shopping woes might not resonate with my current audience. But, as I felt myself sinking into a deep mire of self-serving shallowness, the Lord, or maybe my finely-honed skill of avoiding suffering, threw me a lifeline.

"Actually, Vos, I'm just an outsider, and I'd really like to observe how you lead." Even as the words came out of my mouth, I felt happy feelings. I may have even added that observing Vos lead was all part of getting a bigger picture for the staff selection process.

Vos switched into the Tajik language to lead a short Bible lesson followed by the sharing of more prayer requests. I breathed a sigh of relief. We drank some tea, ate a bit of stale flatbread and made our way back to the door to scale the iceberg that led up to the road.

I couldn't wait to get back into the Neva, in hope that the jeep's heater actually functioned. The mountain air was just above freezing, and the temperature in Banu's living room was the same. Yet, between myself and the Neva, forming a blockade of cuteness, stood four elementary school girls dressed in T-shirts, paper-thin leggings, headscarves, and rubber galoshes that rose to mid ankle with no socks. Each of the girls had a slightly different shade of mysterious green-yellow eyes, enchanting in the truest sense of the word. They beamed wide smiles and began thanking Vos and our group for coming to the village.

As we sputtered off, I twisted in my seat to watch the Tajik beauties wave goodbye until we were around the first switchback down the mountain. I asked Vos how he had initially surfaced interest for a Bible study in this entirely Muslim village. He slowly turned to me, keeping one eye on the hazardous road, and smiled with his entire face.

"I knew that Jesus cared about these people, but I didn't have a great strategy for reaching them. So I just started driving up here once a week and knocking on doors. I would ask if I could pray for whoever was home and for any problems they had. Everyone had problems, so everyone let me pray for them. One time, God decided to heal someone I was praying for, and within days, every other family in the village heard about it. After that, it was easy to gather people for Bible study."

We bounced along the road for another 20 minutes to the next village. More open doors, more tea, more flatbread, more accounts of suffering, and more testimonies of answered prayer. Stories about Jesus's love, care and provision seemed to ring from the village-laden Tajik mountain tops, in large-part due to one person's faithfulness.

The sun dropped behind the rugged peaks and rose the following day as I boarded my plane back home. I had come to conduct an interview, and as often occurs, God had something bigger in mind. God rekindled the joy of focusing on others and honoring their needs above my own. He reminded me that the really important things involve people, giving, and taking chances to serve others. God also reminded me that He has prepared good works for us all to walk into, and sometimes they look like a waste of time.

> "'Wake up, sleeper, rise from the dead, and Christ will shine on you.'Be very careful, then, how you live—not as unwise but as wise, making the most of every opportunity,
> because the days are evil."
> Eph 5:14b-16

REFLECTION

1. What distracts you from pursuing the things you know are most important in life?

2. What can you do to make God's priorities your priorities?

3. How will you get God's priorities into your weekly schedule?

WEDDING PARTY

Day 15 – by Dina

"Bear one another's burdens,
and thereby fulfill the law of Christ."
Gal 6:2

In the early years of student ministry in Kyrgyzstan, Dan helped a young student named Baish entrust his life to Jesus. Only weeks after his decision, Baish brought his girlfriend Dinara to a gathering of believing students. Dinara was bold, straightforward, and self-confident, unlike most reticent Kyrgyz I had met. I could see her mind spinning as students talked about God. When we turned to the Bible, she engaged unreservedly in the verses we read together. Then, unexpectedly, the Holy Spirit chose to move and Dinara insisted we pray for her to receive Jesus right then.

Dinara's decision opened new vistas for both of us. She began to experience a community of love, forgiveness, and reconciled relationships. I discovered the underworld of dormitory life in the university system in Kyrgyzstan.

Central Asian post-soviet dormitories had a culture of their own. No one chose to live in the dormitories, only students from the poorest villages, who didn't have relatives to host them in the capital city, ended up in these holding tanks. The buildings were concrete barracks with little heat, sporadic electricity, and 4-6 students per room. Dorms were markedly devoid of extras, such as lightbulbs and furniture, which immediately vanished from hallways and common areas to be resold at the bazaars. Every dark corner turned into a makeshift latrine for passers-by and the students themselves. Residents would usually bathe once a week at a community bathhouse, which rotated days for receiving women and men. This recipe made for a ripe olfactory sensation when visiting Dinara in her room in order to understand her world and build our friendship.

During one of our weekly appointments, Dinara recalled an incident that took place the week prior when her roommate was home alone. Some young men from another floor of the dorm came banging on doors in the women's wing. The roommate knew what these men wanted as she sat huddled in the corner watching the door rattle. When the three men knocked the flimsy barrier off its hinges, she decided to leap from her third-story window. Dinara's roommate survived the fall but broke both of her legs upon impact. Life for a young lady in the dorms had its hardships. Dinara and other students from the dorm would often stop by our home to take showers, eat home-cooked meals, and relax for a bit in safety.

As Baish and Dinara grew in their love for Jesus, they also grew in their love for each other. This created its own set of problems. Baish was from a devoutly Muslim farming village in Uzbekistan just over Kyrgyzstan's southern border, and Dinara came from a nominally Muslim family in Kyrgyzstan's mountainous north. Baish's grandfather had been a well-respected Mosque leader. Village culture dictated that Baish return to his hometown, marry a local girl, and carry on his Muslim heritage. Baish's father had already hand-picked five acceptable potential brides. Baish's duty was simply to choose one of them, like picking through a pile of ripe watermelons at the market. The father would then make all the needed wedding arrangements that followed. But Baish chose Dinara, a northern girl with a mind of her own.

News reached Baish's father that his son refused to choose a specimen from the preordained harem. Even worse, Baish had forsaken the Muslim faith. Since rumors were circulating in Central Asia that foreigners were paying Muslims to turn to Christianity, Baish's dad offered to double whatever price Baish had received. Again refusal. This necessitated that family ties had to be severed to save face. The father announced to siblings, aunts, uncles, and cousins that he officially disowned Baish as his son and would not attend his wedding. In a communal culture where family means identity, status, and social security, this was devastating.

We watched at a distance as Baish processed the news that he no longer had family nor home to receive him the next time he returned. Since neither Baish nor Dinara had any resources to organize a wedding or secure an independent home, family rejection put marriage plans on hold as well. How could wedding plans proceed with no community to share their blessing and help lift the financial load?

One evening, as our Bible study group prayed for this couple, the students themselves decided that they were Baish and Dinara's new family. The students created a network of believers who committed to bringing a portion of the wedding dinner. Such an undertaking required 45 pounds of rice, 20 pounds of lamb and similarly large quantities of carrots, onions, tea, sweets, and a variety of salads. We also needed a home with a courtyard to host the 100-plus student guests we expected. God, in his abundance provided it all.

On such occasions, the first plate of food is served not to the wedding couple but to the honored parents. The most honored guests sit in the main room, cross legged on the floor, at the far end of a long decorative rectangular tablecloth. Hand-torn pieces of flat bread adorn the eating area. A large circular dish of plov formed the centerpiece. Plov is a Central Asian rice dish with lamb, carrots, onions, cumin and garlic, piled high like a steaming aromatic festive mountain. Nuts and dried apricots filled small plates up and down the adorned piece of cloth. Dinara's parents had come from the north, a grueling 7-hour bus ride away, so they received the culinary honors.

However, as loaded plates moved their direction, a murmur of chatter wafted through the door of the banquet room. Someone had come, someone important, which sent nervous student servers scurrying to their stations. Baish's father bowed his tall Kyrgyz headwear as he entered the room. His countenance was quiet, stoic, and dignified. Did he sense he was the awaited guest of honor, as if he had never disowned his son? Or was he ashamed of his former tirade, yet putting off an air of confidence? Did he consider the burden of broken family relationships heavier than the humility of swallowing his empty threats? His icy gaze around the room gave away no hints at his inner thoughts.

Kyrgyz students in hushed whispers set a plate and utensils so close to Dinara's parents that they had no choice but to surrender at least a portion of their honored position. The young wedded couple, the in-laws, and the entire student population locked eyes on Baish's father. His presence indicated blessing instead of the former curse, a change of heart, a miracle. Baish had risked losing his family by holding to his convictions, yet the prodigal father had returned. His presence spoke volumes.

Introductions were made, the atmosphere lightened, happy conversation intertwined with dancing in the small dimly lit courtyard. The lingering aroma of boiled lamb and steamed dumplings made its way through the crowd. The samovar steamed out boiling water into teapots which circled the room. The wedding celebration signified much more than two young hearts made one. It was a night when the hard ground of Islamic tradition was slightly softened by Christ's love as seen in simple students who had chosen to serve one another. A new generation was springing to life in Central Asia, a generation characterized by kindness, joy, and love, rather than separation and pride.

The day Baish and Dinara were married we proclaimed the dawn of a new generation; the first modern generation of Christ-following families in Kyrgyzstan.

"Bear one another's burdens,
and thereby fulfill the law of Christ."
Gal 6:2

REFLECTION

1. How has your local church or other believers helped you in your spiritual growth?

2. How does your local church help meet physical needs in your community?

3. How might you lighten the burden of someone in need this month?

BABOS

Day 16 – by Dina

> "Truly I tell you," Jesus replied, "no one who has left home or
> brothers or sisters or mother or father or children or fields for
> me and the gospel will fail to receive a hundred times as much
> in this present age: homes, brothers, sisters, mothers, children
> and fields—along with persecutions—
> and in the age to come eternal life."
> Mark 10:29-30

Living on the fifth-floor of a Soviet apartment building with no
elevator wasn't so bad initially. Even though our neighbors complained
about the pounding boots of myriad visiting students echoing in the
stairwell, we felt perched above the daily din of the city, with a bit of fresh
air out our windows to clear our minds. But shortly after the birth of Jack,
our first son, I faced a high-rise dilemma. Upon returning from the outdoor
market, I needed to choose between leaving my child, or the stroller, or the
groceries unattended at the bottom of the stairwell while I ran the other
two upstairs. This daily experiment in risk-management became tedious
and distressing.

Choosing to move away from apartment living and into a home with
a yard was a difficult decision. Our featureless block building in the city
center along with two identical perpendicular units created a partially
enclosed courtyard where kids would play, grandmas would stroll, and the
occasional drunk would pass out. We had shown the Jesus Film in that
courtyard. We celebrated Jack's first birthday in that courtyard, complete
with a slaughtered lamb, traditional contests, and more than 100 neighbors
in attendance. We knew the bread man, the milkman, and every other
vendor within a four-block radius. We knew the evening voices of all the
women calling for their children to come eat dinner and the rhythmic
beating of carpets being cleaned while draped over rusty playground
equipment. Life in the courtyard had become home. Underwear-clad kids

squirting hoses in summer gave way to piles of raked leaves in fall and occasional snowmen, crooked and gray, in the winter. Leaving our two-bedroom apartment atop our now familiar courtyard community came with real sacrifice.

Yet, our move to the neglected house just blocks from the Kyrgyz National University held treasures unforeseen. A few days after moving, during a stroll with Jack down our block, a sturdy, self-confident Tatar* woman stepped out in front of the stroller. Her jolly round face beamed kindness. With a voice as sweet as sugar, she greeted us in English, "Hello, How are you? Welcome to Ofisersky" (the name of our quiet narrow alley tucked between two busier avenues). This was just what I needed to soothe my worried heart about all the relationships I felt I had left behind. Sweet-voiced Elmira held the hand of her 4-year-old grandson Timur. "This is Tima," she sung like a high-pitched songbird. I felt as if I could float on the serenity of her voice.

"And this is Jack," I replied. The two brown-headed boys with bowl haircuts looked one another over shyly but curiously.

"We are so glad to have new neighbors," Elmira melodied. "We have two boys who would love to play with Jack." These were words a young mom delights to hear. I was already concerned that Jack's social life, at two years old, would be forever scarred after leaving our courtyard friends.

"Oh, we would like that," I answered earnestly.

Jack had a hard time saying many names at this point. Elmira Sharipovna Hafizova was definitely beyond range. In her gentle accommodating way, Elmira immediately requested to be called "Babo," an endearing Russian term for grandmother. As Jack tried to repeat "Babo" he successfully spit out "Babos" with a lingering "s" on the end. We all laughed and smiled at his effort, but the term "Babos" stuck permanently.

Babos and I became inseparable over time. We spent long mornings together drinking tea as Tima and Jack ran around the house laughing and periodically passing through the kitchen to grab a hot piece of bread from the table. I absorbed language and culture as Babos would share of her life and history over sips of tea and mouthfuls of jam.

* Turkic Muslims of Ukraine and Russia

She grew up in Kizil Kia, Kyrgyzstan among the rolling foothills along the border of Tajikistan. In order to get a more formal education in the Russian language, Elmira and her brother daily hitchhiked 12-miles across the border to the nearest school in Tajikistan. Rides usually came from merchants entering Kyrgyzstan to meet trains full of imported wares. The route took more than an hour each way, standing in the back of open-bed trucks, bouncing through potholes and gradually being coated in a layer of road dust.

In the years that followed, Elmira married a classmate named Rafael. Rafael was born in Russia, during the reign of Stalin. Seven days after Rafael's birth, his father was accused of being an enemy of the state and was executed immediately by a firing squad. Since such accusations tended to snowball throughout extended families, despite a complete absence of substantiating evidence, Rafael's mother gathered her children and fled to the relative safety and obscurity of Central Asia. Years later, Soviet authorities exonerated Rafael's father as "not-guilty" in a tiny newspaper article which listed the names of innocent victims killed for crimes they didn't commit. This common occurrence under Stalin's watch shaped the worldview and resulting behavior of Rafael's hardened and wary generation.

Elmira and Rafael had only one child, Ildar, who proved to be intelligent, responsible, and ultimately the family's means to upward mobilization. Elmira, by now a teacher and educational leader for the southern region of Kyrgyzstan, was the only English speaker in her corner of the planet. She taught Ildar to speak English as well, so when an American Peace Corps worker arrived to initiate development projects in the area, Ildar was his first hire. Ildar's language and people skills soon propelled the family to Kyrgyzstan's capitol city of Bishkek right about the time our family made our new home there as well.

My hours spent with Babos filled me with wonder...

"When preparing for guests, skillfully shave the block of butter into small delicate curls.
Never serve tea to a guest from a chipped cup.

91

Fill guests' cups with just enough tea for one drink. When they drink, fill it again.

When you offer something from a tray or plate lower your body so that they are above you, this shows humility and gives honor. In your lower position, put the tray forth with your right hand, holding your left hand palm open near your heart. In this way, you're offerings are coming straight from your heart.

Never throw away bread. Bread is holy for the Kyrgyz - a representation of life. Wheat from the field grows to nurture man. We kiss the bread before we break it and eat it. If it is not all consumed, put it in a bag and hang it on a branch for the birds. Never, never, never let it touch the ground."

Babos and I spent hours on our knees working with the soil, prepping it for life giving seeds...

"Take the dirt, sift it with your fingers as you would flour. When it is as fine as powder it is ready. Make enough room for your seed to not be cramped. Only then, gently spread your fine soil over the life."

My ears were perked, taking it all in. It all made perfect sense, gently carry life and help it survive. Any inquiries were welcomed by Babos, and met with with a song-like rhythm that grew me.

About a year after our transition to Ofisersky we were met with some exciting, yet anxiety building news. Ildar and Rushana won the American immigration lottery! They were given a year to make their way to America and get a green card, randomly selected from thousands of applications. The twist was that they could only move as a nuclear family, their parents would remain behind. Ildar and Rushana would need to spend five years in the US before they could become citizens and invite their parents to join them.

The loss of Ildar, Rushana and the boys was almost more than we could bare. We had just acclimated to our new friends and neighborhood. I had no curious aunts or relatives near to inquire about Jack's lost teeth or his first day in the barber's chair. It was quickly decided that Babos and Dedos would move in with us. We sold Ildar's car and built a one bedroom studio next to our house for our Tatar Grandma and Grandpa.

 The addition of Babos and Dedos to our home as an integral part of our everyday lives was a blessing much greater than I had imagined. I had been aching for a grandma to dote on my children and a grandpa to shuffle around and make our lives full with his lessons and quirky old ways. Babos walked newborn Levi in the afternoons around the labyrinth of pot-holed streets and small kiosks that made up our city block. Meanwhile, I went to the university to meet new students.

Dedos had his own investment in my life. He grumbled about how much space in my yard I devoted to flowers, when potatoes and cabbage could occupy the land. But Babos and I would laugh amongst ourselves, because potatoes weren't necessarily worth laboring over. Nevertheless, we eventually conceded a portion of the yard for Dedos' beloved potatoes. They were so small the first year that he plopped them in a kettle of oil and fried them up like doughnut holes. We popped the hot crunchy morsels greedily into our mouths. We praised Dedos for these tasty delights that made for a perfect treat. He smiled as he watched the kids and me eagerly gulp them down. Satisfied and successful, he would walk away with a happy chuckle to return to his potato patch and dig up some more.

When Dan travelled outside the city, Babos and Dedos filled the empty space. Our neighborhood's electricity, spotty at best, drained to a brown minimum in winter. Dedos kept the home fires burning and heated our water on an outdoor fire when needed. On occasion, he put on his gloves and shimmied up the electricity pole to mess with wires and scrutinize the transformer down the street. Neighborhood men would gather at the base of the pole squawking unwanted advice as we watched our 70-year-old grandpa tamper with his life. The lights would flicker, sparks would fly, and we would all hold our breath with concern for the outcome.

I cannot deny that I was absent from moments in my own family's lives that I cannot replace or say I have a memory of — weddings and vows missed, memorials and celebrations forgone. There were a multitude of nieces and nephews I wasn't at the hospital to greet or watch take their first steps. Many "firsts" and "lasts" that I can never say I saw or experienced with people I have loved the bulk of my life. I envied kindergartens with slides and yards with grass. I grieved the idea that baseball, hot dogs, and apple pie were not a part of our vocabulary or experience. But days in our courtyard living on top of one another, and years with Babos and Dedos and neighbors that lined the hole-pocked street of Ofisersky, were of no less importance.

Faces of my neighborhood sift through my mind reminding me of God's provision and promises. Etched on my heart are neighborhood children - Marina and Roma pushing sleds down the street; Aunt Luba selling hard sour yogurt balls through a window in her gate; young Yura mixing chemical concoctions to revive our dead car battery, skills which he learned in the Soviet army now being put to the test; elderly Vera who sewed our Christmas stockings in a flash and would share tulip bulbs from her garden; Svetlana Mihailovna's encouragement and stern medical advice; her handsome boys Dima and Volodya faithfully by her side; and finally Sherik a bubbly, round, smiling Kyrgyz boy outside our gate yelling "Jacky let's jump," in a high pitched lyric.

The Lord promised more and he gave more — not better, not complete, but a life of love and laughter, knitting our souls with those across land and sea. Timeless tongues and cultures have procured a memory of my other family — the family I would've never met or experienced if we had said, "No" to God's call to settle in a distant land, not insulated by common things, routine and the predictable.

"Truly I tell you," Jesus replied, "no one who has left home or brothers or sisters or mother or father or children or fields for me and the gospel will fail to receive a hundred times as much in this present age: homes, brothers, sisters, mothers, children and fields—along with persecutions— and in the age to come eternal life."
Mark 10:29-30

REFLECTION

1. How have you seen Mark 10:29-30 worked out in your life?

2. For many of us, family may not fulfill our needs for love and belonging. How do you think God can fulfill the needs our families may have failed to meet?

3. How does the promise of eternal life put our current needs in perspective?

PORTABLE HOLIDAY

Day 17 – by Dan

"In everything I did, I showed you that by this kind of hard work we must
help the weak, remembering the words the Lord Jesus himself said:
'It is more blessed to give than to receive.'"
Acts 20:35

Although the perks of urban living under Soviet communism were
few and far between, those who grew up in cities throughout the Russian-
controlled empire speak nostalgically of the stability communism provided.
Comrades from St. Petersburg to Vladivostok knew that Big Brother would
provide bread, electricity, and central heating at least in city centers. For
those outside the radius of underground piping, mother Russia subsidized
coal prices to stoke primitive metal cylinders that oozed heat into the
primary room of each rural home.

Another communist peculiarity was workplace comradery. Not only
did school teachers see each other at work, but entire apartment buildings
were dedicated to house those same teachers the other 16 hours of the
day. Furniture factory workers could all ride the same public bus home and
walk into the same gated courtyard at the center of three "U" shaped high-
rise concrete boxes before dispersing into their government issued two-
room apartments. Military officers were issued identical quarter-acre plots
of land along a pot-holed alley as appreciation for their service to the
greater good.

It was just such an alley where we took up residence after outgrowing
our central soviet apartment. Not surprisingly, the narrow street was
named "Officer's Alley". Our home in the middle of the block came to be
the hub of activity for neighborhood children and adults alike. We built a
play structure in our yard and even commandeered a full-sized trampoline
off some exiting foreigners. Our home hosted karaoke nights, costume
parties, Easter egg hunts, and multiple birthdays complete with Piñatas
(which should be mandatory for all cultures worldwide). Each Wednesday

afternoon interested neighbors entered our gate to participate in an exploratory Bible study. Regular attenders included doctors and nurses, translators, television talk-show hosts, seamstresses, jewelry makers, and car mechanics. Oh, yes, and one cleaning lady name Aigulya.

Aigulya was a single mother of two. Aibek, her son, was an intelligent boy of ten, and Elmira, her daughter, was six when Aigulya began attending our study. Aigulya's husband had left shortly after Elmira was born with cerebral palsy. Mom and kids lived at the end of Officer's Alley in what should have been a condemned shack. The tenuous mud-brick dwelling consisted of two rooms connected by the aforementioned coal-burning metal cylinder. I was familiar with the layout of Aigulya's home because during one cold December Wednesday study, Aigulya mentioned that her furnace was backed up with soot and no longer usable. Yura the jeweler and I spent the following evening unclogging chimney pipes and inhaling Zoolander proportions of coal dust. Elmira smiled at us from her wheelchair, and Aibek helped his mom serve us tea and bread.

Each week day Aigulya would leave the house at 6:00 a.m. and place a padlock on the outside of the entry door to keep her children safe inside. She boarded a well-used soviet trolley bus that chattered up Peace Prospect to the polytechnic university where she scrubbed dormitory floors and unspeakable squat toilets until returning home by 6:00 p.m. Aibek and Elmira dutifully entertained themselves for the 12-hour workday without the luxury of TV, personal electronic devices, toys, or fresh air.

Elmira's smile was etched in my mind after that day of chimney sweeping, so I started pondering how our family might help, even if we couldn't solve everything painful about the situation. I also pondered Paul's admonition in Acts 20:35, "In everything I did, I showed you that by this kind of hard work we must help the weak, remembering the words the Lord Jesus himself said: 'It is more blessed to give than to receive.'" Could it really be true that giving is better than receiving? I reflected on all the fun gifts I had received as a child. It was hard to fathom what Jesus was thinking when he elevated the giving above the getting. Nevertheless, the Christmas season was again upon us, and after a quick brainstorming session with my wife, we decided on a New Year surprise strategy for Aigulya.

Since the Soviets did away with Christmas (and other expressions of religion) under the heading "opiate of the masses,"[vii] the New Year celebration replaced Jesus' birthday as the bright spot in otherwise long gray winters. New Year's festivities included Yolkas (otherwise known as Christmas trees), ornaments, gifts, and large meals usually spent with vodka-drinking uncles and reruns of traditional Soviet films on TV.

Our family, however, despite almost a decade in former Soviet republics, just couldn't get December 25th out of our system. We traditionally began celebrating Christmas the day after Thanksgiving, regardless of where we were living. And, since live "New Year" trees only went on sale around December 23rd or 24th, we were relegated to the ranks of fake-tree owners. This way, we could blast Christmas carols, admire twinkling tree lights, and slowly accumulate gifts under the artificial tree for the entire month of December.

The New Year surprise strategy for Aigulya proposed that we celebrate Christmas as a family at our home on December 25th, then transport a real tree, lights, ornaments, presents and lots of cheer to Aigulya's house on December 31st, just in time for New Year.

This all looked great on paper until it started to snow. December 31st began with a cold, wet downfall that covered the city. Temperatures dropped throughout the day as the snowfall grew heavier. In addition, I briefly forgot about the Aigulya plan in the midst of Christmas parties, New Year's festivities, and lots of guests in our home. Therefore, about 6 p.m. on the 31st, I brewed up a fresh pot of decaf and settled into my favorite chair to wind down from the day and read a good book. Just as I took my first sip of dark elixir, my much-less-forgetful wife announced that in five minutes we were loading up and heading out. Everything in me rebelled. As I started to compose my list of excuses (snow, darkness, cold, the potential of my coffee losing its optimum flavor), Paul's words surfaced in my memory:

"I showed you that by this kind of hard work we must help the weak, remembering the words the Lord Jesus himself said: 'It is more blessed to give than to receive.'"

Maybe serving others wasn't supposed to be easy or convenient, and could I really believe that Jesus had something better than a nice cup of coffee on the other side of this effort?

The next thing I knew, I was bundled in a parka carrying a fully decorated tree above my head and walking through six inches of snow down Officer Alley. The pine needles poked my eyes and head and hands. Our four small children struggled to make headway while expressing all the complaints I had rehearsed back in my coffee chair.

Aigulya's face beamed as we crossed the threshold. Elmira poked her head around the corner and started to giggle with excitement. Aibek, however, just stared at us with a blank look on his face. I didn't pay much attention since I was busy pulling pine needles out of my neckline. When the tree was finally in place, lights plugged into their one and only electrical outlet, and presents placed with the precision of a craftsman, I once again looked around at the recipients of our efforts. Aigulya was in awe, Elmira couldn't stop smiling and Aibek, with a polite but disturbed expression, kept whispering something to his mom. I finally asked, "What's going on? Is everything okay with Aibek?"

"Yes," said Aigulya. "He's just having a hard time believing what he's seeing."

"Why is that?," I asked

Aigulya went on to explain what had transpired earlier that day. "Shortly after waking up this morning, Aibek asked me why God had forgotten us." When she asked what he meant, he said, "All my friends get gifts every New Year, but I have never received a gift in my life. So, I think God has forgotten us."

Aigulya tried to assure Aibek that this was not the case, but she also knew that she had no means to fix the gift situation herself, nor offer Aibek any material proof that God was, indeed, looking after all their needs. So she suggested that the two of them pray that God would show He hasn't forgotten them by somehow providing a gift for the New Year. Eight hours later, through some prompting of the Spirit and my considerate wife, God led us through their door with bags full of presents.

Fifteen years have passed since God used my reluctant efforts to convince a ten-year-old that He is real, and that He hears and cares. God also convinced a middle-aged doubter that it really is better to give than to receive, because by doing so, we may get to take part in plans unseen that have been set into motion by God and await our participation.

> In everything I did, I showed you that by this kind of hard work we must help the weak, remembering the words the Lord Jesus himself said:
> 'It is more blessed to give than to receive.'"
> Acts 20:35

REFLECTION

1. When do you have a hard time believing it is better to give than to receive?

2. When have you felt fulfilled after giving to someone or meeting someone else's need?

3. An old Scottish Bible teacher used to tell me that God is the most blessed of all beings, therefore, He will always give more than He receives. Hence, we can never outgive God. Have you seen this to be true in your experience? How?

TWO TRUTHS AND A LIE
Day 18 – by Dina

> "Does a spring of water bubble out with both fresh water and
> bitter water? Does a fig tree produce olives,
> or a grapevine produce figs?
> No, and you can't draw fresh water from a salty spring.
> If you are wise and understand God's ways, prove it by living an
> honorable life, doing good works with the humility
> that comes from wisdom."
> James 3 : 11-13

There are days I am convinced that the Lord is shining through me, radiant for all to see. Other days, I want to hide under a rock.

After 19 years of field ministry with students, teachers and communities, Dan and I moved into a role of regional leadership. One of my colleagues on the area team, Mike, said he had crossed paths with some old college friends who knew me from my years in Central Asia. He mentioned some familiar names. I traced back 15 years, remembered their faces and the shipping business they started that helped us receive care packages while living abroad. Warm fuzzy feelings pervaded.

Then Mike began to laugh and said he had learned something interesting about me. At that point, I realized I had left a long-lasting impression on my long-lost acquaintances that was possibly embarrassing. With fear and trembling, I urged Mike to share their comments.

He quoted the wife's remark, "I'll never forget what Dina said when we played a game called 'Two Truths and a Lie.'" Then the memories flooded in...

"Two Truths and a Lie," is a game we often played with students to break the ice. The idea is to share three personal facts, two of which are true and the other is a lie. This particular evening I had a group of expatriate women to my home for a book study and maybe because the conversation was already on the topic of struggles with living cross-culturally, I blurted out my three claims:

"I hit a Kyrgyz, I kicked a Kyrgyz, and I spit on a Kyrgyz."

Puzzled looks came over the faces of the civilized women in our discussion group, some with USAID, others doing medical reform, and a spattering of workers from various mission organizations. It was a group of women mature in faith, utterly compassionate and sacrificial as they lived their lives abroad for the sake of others. I must say it was the "cream of the crop" when it came to women of character, the type of crowd anyone would want to rub shoulders with. I felt like a better person just being around these ladies. But what did I just say? I had just exposed my dark side. How could any of those things be true of one of God's servants? I had their attention; their eyes begged explanation.

It was winter in Bishkek, cold icy streets lured vendors to take to the underground passageways to display their wares. I had my family visiting for the first time, and we set out on an excursion of the capital. In a crowded underpass, my brother, Johnny, took interest in some commotion taking place with a street hustler and a guessing game. He unwittingly began pointing at the cups which he thought were covering the hidden walnut. Passers-by began to pause and fill the area to watch this foreigner get fooled by the street-seasoned Kyrgyz "artist."

As the crowd formed a circle around my brother, I realized that he had unknowingly become the spectacle of this gambling game. The audience continued to grow to a large mob in the underpass. We were in a mess and before I could stop what was happening the cups moved and my brother had guessed wrongly. The Kyrgyz ring-leader immediately honed in on Johnny. In Russian, he blurted out his demand for payment, then grabbed money out of my brother's hand as Johnny stood dumfounded. My body turned hot with adrenalin as Johnny got "juked" by this sly guy! Before the hustler stepped away with the wad of cash he had snatched from Johnny's hand, I lunged toward him and slapped his hard winter-weathered face. I grabbed the money from his clenched fist, and yelled at my brother to run. With a stinging palm, I pushed Johnny through the underground crowd, and yanked my mom behind me with my heart pounding as shame ensued from my gut.

This was my new community, the streets I daily strolled for bread and potatoes. Each morning I greeted the bread man and brought my empty jars out to be filled by the milk man. I regularly bought gum and popcorn from the round toothless Babushka who occupied the first step. More than 100 neighbors and vendors attended my first child's birthday party in the courtyard we shared. But here in the underpass I lashed out and violated a representative of the very people I came to serve. And here was my mother, father, and brother visiting us for a few short days to see our lives and service in the country.

Life hit hard that day, in more ways than one.

Then there was the second truth to reveal...

It was a warm sunny day in spring when we invited our neighbors over for their first Easter celebration. We were excited to share our holiday traditions with the kids and the message of God's love through Jesus to three local families we had befriended. We usually waited to buy bread until guests were close to arriving so that it would be hot out of the fiery clay tandir oven nearby. When the time was right, I sped up the street to our local bread vendor.

As I walked back with arms stacked high of steaming flat bread, a group of young gypsy boys encircled me. One was reaching into my pockets, another grabbing bread and still another was jabbing me from behind laughing because I had no free hand to ward him off. The bread load had me incapacitated. Frustration rushed through my body like fire, my mind raced to find a solution to this offense. My stern reprimand made no difference to the boys. They continued to poke and jab. Before I could give it a moment of thought, I dug deep from my throat, hacking up as much saliva as I could. A shower of spit came raining down on the gypsy parade encircling me. As the children fled, I tried to gain composure. Shamefully, I began looking around to see who had witnessed Dina in full color. I stood alone, face flushed hot with disgrace, reflecting on what I had done. Who had I become? I walked back home to host the "fortunate ones" in my life, but all the while, my conscience was chained to the nagging vision of spitting on street children that sacred Easter morning.

How do I begin to explain hitting or spitting on anyone? Couldn't I have just blessed those wayward children with fresh bread and gone back for more? Why was I so concerned about my brother losing face and a few dollars to a slithery street vendor trying to make a living with a simple illusion of moving cups and walnuts? Is it really worth taking away someone 's dignity by hitting them in the face or spitting on their head? The confessions of a missionary need to be made. My mission had gone south. Though I had fed, clothed, housed, and led people toward the love of God, I had a continual battle within myself. I wanted justice, respect, and not to be taken advantage of! I'm flesh and blood--a compilation of inner frustrations and disappointments--shocked by my own behavior.

The New Testament book of James points out that from the same spring we cannot draw clean and polluted water. Without the power of the Holy spirit in my life I will constantly be drawing from myself, which only produces what I am able to give and inevitably falls short of the best. Either I will appear kind hearted, but be harboring anger inside, or I will display my anger for all the world to see. Only by the power of the Spirit will I be harnessed and refined. My journey continues daily, humbling me to see my need for God's grace and power. When victories are experienced, and patience and kindness result, I am reminded that there is a God committed to the transformation of my heart!

It is true that I'm not the perfect person for this job. It's true that I still may not know what it means to "love" my neighbor. It is true that I hit a Kyrgyz street merchant and spit on impoverished gypsy children. My insecure, flustered, annoyed self got the best of me. It took all of me to step out in faith and believe that possibly the Lord could still grow me and possibly use me to impart something better to the community in which I lived. In God's graciousness, He has redeemed so many of my ugly moments and used them to transform me and others. I rejoice in His mercy and kindness.

I also rejoice in the fact that I stumped the ladies in the book study and I can honestly testify that I have not once "kicked" a Kyrgyz. That is the lie, because I'd never do that...well, probably not.

> "Does a spring of water bubble out with both fresh water and
> bitter water? Does a fig tree produce olives,
> or a grapevine produce figs?
> No, and you can't draw fresh water from a salty spring.
> If you are wise and understand God's ways, prove it by living an
> honorable life, doing good works with the humility
> that comes from wisdom."
> James 3 : 11-13

REFLECTION

1. In what ways do you feel unworthy or unqualified to be used by God?

2. Read through a list of character qualities that God desires to produce in His followers (I Tim 3:2-10) What quality would you like to be truer of your character?

3. How can you imagine God using even your shortcomings to glorify Himself?

THE CORE EVENT
Day 19 – by Dan

"And the things you have heard me say in the presence of many
witnesses entrust to reliable people
who will also be qualified to teach others."
2 Tim 2:2

After eight years of conducting college student discos, beauty pageants, street-ball tournaments, and park-bench conversations in Central Asia, our original team of five Americans and two Kyrgyz had multiplied into six ministry teams in four different cities. The most recent expansion occurred in the overgrown village of Jalalabad on Kyrgyzstan's southern border with Uzbekistan. Jalalabad State University enrolled more than 4000 students -- students who were looking for opportunities to socialize, compete, make friends, and expand their horizons. In August we organized a team of five Kyrgyz and Russian staff to see if they could make inroads into the student population and assess their spiritual interest. Sasha and his wife Nuria agreed to leave their home in the capital city for a year and lead the team into new territory. This was Sasha's first attempt at team leadership, but both he and Nuria led forth with enthusiasm and courage to mobilize this small band of men and women.

Almost immediately upon arrival the team began meeting university officials, hosting student parties, and generating contact with students refreshingly unspoiled by urban commercialism. During September and October, the new team saw several students start their journey as followers of Jesus and form a small weekly Bible study. By the time I visited in November, 25 students rallied each week, either to grow spiritually or to explore why all these other students were talking about Jesus.

One afternoon in the middle of my three-day stopover, Sasha hosted me to an outdoor shish kebab stand with a giant pig's head in a bucket out front. I guess the pig's head was a warning for devout Muslims and a siren's call for the rest of us. It's hard to beat hot pork on a stick.

However, the post-meal layer of grease and onion garnish can only be flushed away with a nice pot of tea, so Sasha led me to a surprisingly western looking coffee shop run by some like-minded Canadians who wanted to create a small refuge of hot beverage and conversation in the midst of Jalalabad's dusty streets.

As we stepped into the coffee shop, two of Sasha's friends were waiting for him on the couch. The two young men, Vova and Igor, embraced Sasha with a hug, introduced themselves and sat us down around a   pot of tea. I began asking questions about how each of them originally met Sasha and soon came to find out that Vova was already a believer in Jesus and Igor was still searching. Sasha used me as an excuse to reengage Igor in another explanation of Jesus' payment for sin and God's desire to relate to us as Father and friend.

At this point I felt like I was transported a little bit off into the distance and could observe the whole event as if I was hovering above it, kind of like Bart Simpson's out-of-body experience. I made a mental snapshot of the magical moment and determined that this was the true essence of ministry. Paul's discipleship challenge to Timothy in 2 Timothy 2:2 was captured in this single event. I theorized that Sasha's coffee shop conversation depicted the fundamental behavior for building movements of multiplying disciples. A three-person interaction (disciplemaker, disciple, and non-believer) was etched in my memory and in time became known in the ministries we led as the Core Event.

What was taking place in this episode that would prompt us to give it an official title?

1) The Core Event demonstrates life-on-life discipleship. Similar to Jesus in Mark 3:14, the disciplemaker is asking the disciple be with him or her, modeling evangelism, so he or she can later send them out to preach. Christian growth has moved from reading a book over a cup of tea and discussing its relevance to taking a step of faith to influence the world.

2) The Core Event demonstrates evangelism. New people are invited to consider God's kingdom, Jesus' invitation, and to experience the hope of eternal life. The Core Event helps fulfill Jesus' command to go and make disciples of all nations.

3) The Core Event promotes leadership development. Meeting new people takes planning, initiative, and evaluation to increase effectiveness. Ideally, the disciplemaker builds these skills into the disciple as they together commit themselves to a Core Event strategy. The disciplemaker models, then passes leadership on to the disciple. Eventually the disciple takes the lead. The disciplemaker becomes a coach and encourager.

Sasha and his buddies on the couch turned into an icon which became posted on our ministry communications and newsletters and weekly evaluation charts. The three stick-figure symbol reminded all our staff of the main task. Weekly scoreboards measured the number of Core Events each ministry team conducted, and what activities were required to set the stage for successful Core Events. In our little regional staff culture, the term 'Core Event' made its way into the four primary languages of our area. All 330 staff knew what specific behavior we believed was essential to build movements of multiplying disciples.

Only after a year of driving the Core Event train into the homes of more than 50 ministry teams under our supervision did I understand what was happening. Really we were just rebranding a ministry strategy that had set the DNA for our entire organization and for my personal spiritual journey.

When I was a second-year student at Colorado State University, Mark, my Bible study leader, took me into the dormitories and asked me to sit and pray as he shared the gospel with a student who had expressed spiritual interest during a campus-wide survey. In those days we didn't have a catchy name for the Core Event. It was simply understood that this was part of the discipleship process. Decades later I tried to capture the concept and name it in order to reestablish its prominence as a tool to drive efforts in evangelism and discipleship.

Now for a bit of closure to the story with Sasha, Vova, and Igor. Igor never did end up placing his trust in Christ. Vova may or may not have used the training so effectively modeled in that coffee shop. Sasha and Nuria moved back to the capital city at the end of that first school year and currently serve in a local church, while running their own small business. In the short term, results seemed less than extraordinary. But on a grander scale, the Core Event concept bore more fruit than Sasha or Vova could have ever imagined. Through refocusing our efforts on this foundational behavior, our ministry teams saw more than 3000 Core Events take place in one year resulting in more than 200 new disciples. And now faithful men and women are passing the torch to a next generation who are qualified to teach others.

"And the things you have heard me say in the presence of many
witnesses entrust to reliable people
who will also be qualified to teach others."
2 Tim 2:2

REFLECTION

1. Regardless of how long we have followed Jesus, God desires us to pass on to others what we've learned. Who are you currently investing in or would you like to invest in?

2. List the names of people who might help you grow in your role as a discipler of others.

3. What help do you need to get started in evangelism or discipleship?

Here are some online resources:

http://www.godtoolsapp.com/

https://www.cru.org/train-and-grow/share-the-gospel/evangelism-principles/cojourners.html

http://collegiatecollective.com/author/cru-press-green/

https://www.jesusfilm.org/app

CINDERELLA

Day 20 – by Dina

> "For He has rescued us from the dominion of darkness and
> brought us into the kingdom of the Son he loves"
> Col 1:13

During the tail end of our decade in Kyrgyzstan I had given birth to twin daughters and together with Dan handed off leadership of our ministry organization to competent local colleagues. Both Dan and I felt like God was calling us to another season of overseas ministry so we moved our young family to the Caucuses* and braced ourselves for the next adventure. When we landed on the Absheron peninsula my twin daughters were four years old, Levi was six, and Jack had just turned nine. I was worried about this new placement because I had begun overseas ministry young and vibrant, with no children in tow. In those early days I hit language study hard and it proved to be fruitful. At our first location, by the time my children entered the scene, I had developed so many relationships that there was no need to leave my home to drum up more friends on a university campus. I had students coming out my ears, and neighbors whom I had known from seasons of gathering fruit and vegetables from our gardens and exchanging jam. I already felt a sense of belonging in our neighborhood and city. We were all warm or cold or smashed on public transportation together. Therefore, when I arrived in the Caucuses, I doubted that this new place could ever offer me more depth in relationships than I had already experienced. My standards were high, and my expectations were low.

Yet on one particularly windy day during the intimidating first months of navigating our new city, God whispered to me, "I am the vine and you are the branches. Abide in me and I in you and you will bare much fruit. What do you have to worry about? Remember who you are and stick close to me, Dina!"

*Caucasus - a region at the border of Eastern Europe and Western Asia, situated between the Black Sea and the Caspian Sea.

Shortly thereafter, God proved Himself true to His word. During a going-away party organized by some American students who had spent a gap year in this city. I found myself sticking a Band-Aid onto the leg of an 18-year-old girl named Zola. The American's had met Zola several months earlier when asking directions to the city center. My serendipitous first-aid encounter led to long walks with a new local friend.

On one such stroll in the heat of summer, I pointed to a tea garden in a park. "Let's go sit and have some tea," I suggested.

"Oh, no," Zola replied. "We can't sit there. People would think the wrong thing."

As I inspected the area more closely, sure enough, the only patrons of the tea house were men. Men playing with dice, men smoking, men spitting sunflower seeds at their feet, and men drinking tea. The tea houses and cafes were dominated by males. Only certain types of women dared enter that mix. So, we walked on. We walked for hours past more cafes full of men. This new world wasn't exactly soviet, nor completely Islamic, but it had its own looming oppression.

The hot wind battered us along as I listened to Zola's rugged life journey. Zola had lost both her parents when she was ten years old in a car accident in Russia. She was sent to live with her aunt who had married a man from the Caucuses years earlier and moved to his hometown. Zola grew up assimilating local language and Islamic traditions. As Zola shared her story, I couldn't help but think she was a modern-day Cinderella. Her spoiled cousin, the "step sister," taunted and teased her throughout her teen years. When the family traveled, or went out for the day, they left Zola to stay at home. Each of Zola's birthdays passed uncelebrated, yet she carried the load of housework for the entire family.

Zola seemed undaunted and energetic, flashing her innocent infectious smile. Since she could rarely leave the house, she poured her teenage-enthusiasm into academics and earned a full-ride scholarship to the largest university in the country, along with much recognition from her teachers and school administrators. Therefore, public opinion would have shamed Zola's aunt and uncle had they forbade her to get a higher education. So, with a reluctant family's approval, and the Lord's guiding hand, she entered the university, met some American students, and now we were building an unusual friendship.

When I broached the topic of what she thought about God, Zola replied, "I know that there is a god, and that it is not the god of my aunt and uncle. There is no love in that god." Zola recalled a children's Bible given by a grandmother as the only inheritance she received when her parents passed away. The Bible had pictures with one-page explanations of each story. The pictures left their impression on her mind and soul.

"My image of God is a man opening his arms, rising in the sky, with a look of love on his face. This is what I remember and what I want to be true, but the Bible was taken from me and my aunt never let me have it back," Zola expounded.

We spoke about this image of God during the days that followed; who he was, how much he loved her, and how he really is her Creator. Zola came to life. Her face brightened, eyes twinkling with hope. Her whole body seemed to sit up straight when we conversed about this life-giving God, again like Cinderella dreaming of her prince charming.

One day Zola shared about an experience she had on the subway. She had looked around at all the faces and thought, *They seem like potatoes. Just lifeless, faceless, hard, tasteless potatoes. Isn't that what we are without God?* I couldn't have expressed it better.

In the months that followed, I introduced Zola to several other girls who had professed a faith in Jesus. I knew she needed fellowship besides me. Zola wasn't too keen on this group. She didn't want to offend me or judge others, but she communicated that she didn't feel like these other girls were very serious about their faith. Indeed, these young ladies needed time to grow. I agreed to meet individually with Zola. She would share struggles at home, successes on campus, conflicts with friends, and her thoughts about the Lord. She always seemed to be thinking deeply, with a clear mind and a pure heart.

Nevertheless, circumstances at home grew increasingly wearisome for Zola. She was tired of her role as maid and cook. She was saddened by the absence of invitations to family outings, weddings, and birthday parties. In addition, it seemed like her uncle and aunt were becoming ever more aggressive toward her, especially when they discovered she was pursuing faith in Jesus. There were days when she was forbidden to go to the university. Any of Zola's protests or complaints were met with the back of her uncle's hand.

One night I received a text, "I think tonight I may die. I have been beaten with a chair and can't get up." I texted her and told her I'd come for her. She told me she must leave in the middle of the night when everyone was asleep. She sounded as though she feared for her life.

That night Zola silently held her breath and coaxed her beaten body inch by inch down the dark hallway toward the apartment door. Each squeaky hinge and creaking floorboard seemed miraculously muffled that evening. Straining in the dark to close the heavy metal door behind her without a sound, Zola hurried down the blackened stairwell and into a courtyard where a fellow student's car awaited. He drove her outside the city limits to his older brother's house for the night. Zola called me early the next morning, relieved but still fearful. Although I initially brought her to our home, we realized that within a couple of days the uncle would come looking for her. He knew Zola attended our English program, and it was a matter of time before he would trace her steps to our door. That next day Zola's uncle lined the university entrance with men looking for his fugitive niece. It was finals week and he knew that sooner or later Zola would have to visit the university or risk failing to graduate.

Later that week we found a safe-house for Zola. Once she was settled in there, Zola made some phone calls to contact her professors. One by one each professor relayed that her uncle had come to them asking of her whereabouts. The professors, however, due to Zola's academic work and attitude during the past four years, kept her uncle at bay and gave her full credit for the exams. Zola's prayers, character, and her Heavenly Father's care proved unbeatable. Zola graduated with honors, although in customary fashion for her beleaguered life, she kept in hiding while all her classmates celebrated their commencement.

Months went by and Zola lived in a very tight, closed world. Her relatives were enraged and intent on finding her. We were contacted, our house was watched, and our family was followed.

In the months preceding her escape, Zola had started a relationship with a boy named Elchin. Although Elchin was open to learning more about Jesus, he didn't understand the depth of Zola's faith until she walked through the nightmare with her aunt and uncle. Now Elchin had a front-row seat to see how vital the Lord was to Zola. Her faith wasn't founded on a fascination with the West or a fleeting encounter with an American friend. Tangible and frequent intercession with God gave Zola the strength to walk away from her only home. Undeniable miracles lined Zola's winding path through final exams, graduation, safety, and a new home. Zola's God-guided narrative spurred Elchin to consider the God she served more seriously. Within a few months Elchin became our spiritual brother. We baptized him in a small plastic pool in our yard surrounded by a growing fellowship of believers. Upon returning from his obligatory military service, Elchin asked for Zola's hand in marriage. We gathered their closest friends together with Elchin's family and married the couple on our front patio. Elchin had found the glass slipper and Cinderella was free to set off on a new life with her prince.

Orphaned, ignored, and almost crushed, this young girl found her way straight into her Heavenly Father's arms. Or maybe it was her Father's extended arms that found her? Either way, Zola rose out of the ash heap and claimed her eternal prize, which far outweighed anything this world had to offer. And in a flash (though not seemingly so at the time), a new generation of Christ followers was born in a country dominated by darkness. Elchin and Zola stand grounded and firm to this today. Prayerfully, their children will do the same.

Who could have dreamed such a story? A once upon a time tale of lost parents, evil step-siblings, smothered dreams, daring escapes, prince charming, and eternal kingdoms. God continues to write his epic love saga one redemptive story at a time. In this particular case, he chose to let me step into the drama and observe His masterpiece unfold. How many other tales is God waiting for us to step into if we keep our eyes open and have a spare Band-Aid on hand?

"For He has rescued us from the dominion of darkness and
brought us into the kingdom of the Son he loves"
Col 1:13

REFLECTION

1. Who in your life may be struggling with discouragement, unhealthy relationships, or hopelessness?

2. How can you help move them toward the comfort and hope found in God?

3. What is one practical way to show others a glimpse of the "Kingdom of God?"

THE LITTLE GREEN BOOK
Day 21 – by Dina

> "In his defense Jesus said to them, 'My Father is always at his
> work to this very day, and I too am working.'"
> Jn 5:17

Following my junior year in college, I went on a short-term service trip
to East Asia. My group of ten colleagues studied language at a teachers'
university in a bustling city of 18 million people. We were told that if we
ever talked about our faith it must not be on the university grounds and we
must be very selective as to whom, when, and how we would communicate
with the local people. The purpose of our trip was to help local people have
a chance to hear about a Creator God who loved them. I doubted our small
troupe's efforts could make much of a difference in this mass of humanity
with all our quirky American ways, excessive volume, and obtrusive
behavior.

Throughout the summer I often walked the city with fellow students.
One day as my friend Margaret (so we called her) gave me a tour of her
campus, we ended up chatting in a classroom. Despite a significant
language barrier, we attempted to share what each other studied in college.
I fumbled around trying to find simple words to explain cultural
anthropology.

Fortunately, Harrison Ford's "Indiana Jones" had already spanned the
globe in theatres, so I tried to make the connection with Margaret. I
reasoned that Indiana was similar to an anthropologist, on the hunt for old
artifacts to explain human cultures. I said, "The story is about a man trying
to find the Ark of the Covenant, from ancient Bible times, where the
presence of God was supposed to be."

She immediately hushed her voice, looked to the right and the left of
the empty room and whispered, "You know Bible?"

I nodded my head as if any words might get me in trouble. I looked
to the right and left just as she had done to make sure no eyes were

peeking through the walls. She grabbed my arm, led me outside and walked 100 meters from the building before she spoke again. Once we hit a wooded park she began to tell me her story.

"About three years ago a woman came to my university. She gave me a little green book the size of my hand," Margaret said as she held her palm out. "It is called 'The Holy Bible,' by Gideon." She went on, as if I had never heard of this book before. "I read this book. I read it again and again, because it spoke to my heart like no other book I have ever read. This man Jesus tells us about a kingdom, a kingdom where God is and wants us all to be. I love this God, I love this book. Can you tell me anything more about it?"

The rest of the summer Margaret and I hopped from park to park, sitting under trees reading this little green book together. Her questions were about her future. "What do I do when I graduate and they tell me to sign with the Communist Party? If I sign with the party, I must say I disregard any belief system except for that of the Communist Regime. If I don't sign their document, they will not give me a good job in a good place. They will send me to a far off city away from my family and friends."

"Margaret, I cannot tell you what to do. This is your life. These are your decisions. I can show you many verses in the Bible where these hard decisions were made. But now it is your story and you must choose what you think God wants for you."

After a few more days of reading and discussing the scriptures, Margaret said, "I know what to do, but it will be very hard."

About 5:00 a.m. on the morning of my departure, I got a buzz at the door. The ringing was relentless so I finally got up to see that it was Margaret and Veronica her roommate.

"Dina!" they said with excitement and urgency, "we had to find you and tell you what happened last night." In unison they began interrupting each other, then Margaret won out. "Last night Veronica was paralyzed to her bed, she made a noise and I went to her. Her arms were stuck to her side, her eyes wide open with fear, but no part of her could move. I remembered our conversation about Jesus' power over every other power. I started to pray and tell Jesus I needed his power. I called out his name, even though I was nervous to do it with Veronica. But Veronica looked at me for help. When I said Jesus' name her body started to shake. I knew that Jesus' name was having an influence. I continued to pray for many minutes."

Veronica continued the story, "Finally the pressure left me, my muscles were so sore, but I could feel my arms limp on my bed. All I could think was, 'Who is this Jesus who has more power than whatever paralyzed me?' So, Margaret explained to me that Jesus is more than a man, that he is the one who frees us from spiritual forces and brings us to our heavenly Father who created us. Dina, I know this is true."

I left Asia amazed that the faithfulness of a woman with a little green book had eventually led not only to a disciple, but now also to a disciple maker.

Fast forward four years. I had graduated from the university, gotten married, and gone through several months of cross-cultural training, language school, and moved with my new husband to Bishkek, Kyrgyzstan on the western border of China.

After three months in our host country, I met identical twin sisters at a student gathering. Janara and Nur were 18 years old and studying together at the agricultural university. They were dressed in matching red leggings reaching just below their knees and matching yellow, green, and red shirts that hung below their waists. When we began to share about our views on the meaning of life, I realized they were not like Muslim girls I had met previously. The more I shared about my personal relationship with Jesus, the more the twins exchanged glances with odd curiosity.

When I finally asked what was on their minds, they hesitated. Finally Janara said, "We know this Jesus you are talking about."

"What? I thought that your schools taught Jesus was a fairy tale? And what about your Islamic roots?" My curiosity had overcome any need for subtlety.

"A year ago there was a woman at our university visiting. We didn't know her, but she asked for directions one day on campus and we helped her. Before she left us, she gave us a green book."

Memories of Margaret holding out her hand to show the size of the book flooded my mind.

"Can you tell me what this book looked like?" I asked anxiously.

"A small green book, it is called 'The Holy Bible.' We read it many times."

The blood in my body seemed to rise a few degrees as a warm sensation flowed through me.

"Right after we read the book, we had dreams of a gentle faced man coming to us in light. We knew this book was the reason. We had always prayed to God in our Muslim way, but this is different."

"Are you still reading the book?" I asked.

"Parts of it," Nur replied. "Our mother ripped some of it up. You see, when we were young, our older brother drank a lot with our father and one day hung himself from depression. Then several months ago, my mother had a dream. In the dream, my mother saw us pour boiling water on my brother's head. So when she awoke, she was furious with us. She told us it is because we were betraying our Muslim faith that our brother was suffering beyond the grave. She tore up our little book. But we were desperate for its words. We gathered the pieces of pages she ripped out and tried to memorize them. We wrote out what we could remember in our school books."

During the next ten years, the twins and I became like sisters. Janara and Nur grew in faith, became full-time ministers, married, had children, and began a new generation of Christ followers.

In 2005 we left our home in Kyrgyzstan in search of new opportunities to share Christ's love with those who hadn't yet heard. After nine months of exploration and evaluation, we landed amongst the "hot blooded" people groups of the Caucus mountains. Six months after arrival, we opened an English school that gave us ample access to the energetic and outspoken college students of the capitol city.

Amal was an uncharacteristically quiet girl who gravitated toward the back row of every class. Yet, despite her reticence, she persisted in inviting our family to her home. By this time in our overseas adventures my four kids were tired of being "guests" in cultures where dinners stretch from four to six hours. Our children dreaded the thought of interacting with strangers in another language around a table of unfamiliar food.

Because Amal kept pushing for a date, I finally conceded. We visited her family on a Sunday afternoon following the New Year. To our distraught kids' surprise, several chickens roamed Amal's courtyard pecking around at seeds on the ground. The poultry entertained our disgruntled tribe for the first half hour, but by hour four, it was time to transition into "thank you" and "we really should get going." My first attempt launched us into another hour of small talk because they had yet to serve tea and dessert. The kids sighed, then were slightly fascinated by what came out of the kitchen – a national delicacy – walnuts soaked in jars of sugar water for more than a year. At some point the hard outer shells morph into soft black edible treats served in a pool of syrup, with the appearance of shriveled little brains.

During dessert I learned that Amal's mother was a teacher. Years earlier, an American foundation invited her to attend a conference on education in New York City. Realizing there was no exit until the tea was finished, I said, "Tell me about your experience in America." Amal's mother whispered in her ear and sent Amal off to the back room to retrieve something I assumed would be a photo from her trip. When Amal returned she said, "My mom wants me to ask you about this book she was given. We can't understand it. It is in English but I am having a hard time with it. She handed me a Ziploc bag. Inside it was a small, familiar, green book with gold inscription that said "The Holy Bible."

"Do you know this book Dina? Could you help us understand it?"

Flashbacks of a park outside a Buddhist temple with Margaret blazed through my mind. Memories of my Kyrgyz friends, who had memorized the tiny pages of this book, made my heart pound. And here I sat, a decade later, at a banqueting table with a displaced family from the Caucus region, being asked to *once again* explain a green book's content.

I marveled. My third country and third encounter with this mysterious little book. The Gideon Bible had forged its way into yet another corner of the world. I knew that the Gideon's efforts were vast, but never did I think

121

I'd have three personal encounters over fifteen years with uncanny familiarity. The journey was just as much for me as it was for anyone else.

The ride home from Amal's house was jubilant. Dan and I both reveled in how the Lord weaved together another miraculous tapestry of lives and eternal discoveries. Though the back seat was full of four very tired, complaining, and disgruntled children, I was grateful that the Lord didn't allow me to skirt the invitation for a routine night at home, nor leave prematurely because we didn't have the stamina to last through another cup of tea.

The Lord had been preparing the evening. His plan was much grander than my own. For some odd reason God chooses to involve us in His work. He uses His creation to light up the world for other creations. He is always working, we just need to be obedient to join Him.

> "In his defense Jesus said to them, 'My Father is always at his work to this very day, and I too am working.'"
> Jn 5:17

REFLECTION

1. Where do you see God working around you?

2. How can you join in with God's work?

3. How does the knowledge that God is working (even when we don't see it) affect your emotions?

SAUTÉED RED ONION

Day 22 – by Dan

> "When I kept silent, my bones wasted away through my
> groaning all day long. For day and night your hand was heavy
> on me; my strength was sapped as in the heat of summer. Then
> I acknowledged my sin to you and did not cover up my iniquity.
> I said, 'I will confess my transgressions to the Lord.'
> And you forgave the guilt of my sin."
> Ps 32:3-5

Even if I never read the Bible I would still know something was wrong. By age ten, I had rarely if ever been to church and had no idea what the word "sin" meant, but I could feel the weight of my own corruption. I knew something was awry, that I was behaving in ways I didn't like. Some of my awareness of personal sin came from the mysterious inner workings of my own conscience and some from the look on Mrs. Dawson's face.

Mrs. Dawson was our fifth-grade teacher, and I was the teacher's pet. She was full of creativity, encouragement, a magical reading voice, and everything every fifth-grader wanted in a classroom matriarch. She bragged about my report on Ferdinand Magellan to the rest of the class and made sure I knew about every extra-credit project available. Then one day she gave me what I feared most – the look of utter disappointment, as if I'd broken our year-long teacher-pupil bond of respect.

We had just returned from recess and the daily ritual of mid-morning kickball. I had been appointed one of the captains in charge of choosing teams. After all the good players had been divvied up, I was left with the last kid no one wanted – Daniel. Since kickball was arguably the center of a 10-year-old's universe, I cringed when Daniel stepped up to the plate and threatened our reason for existence. The score was tied and the final recess bell was about to ring. To my amazement and delight, Daniel kicked an uncharacteristically strong grounder past the pitcher and sprinted toward first. He touched first base in plenty of time and my heart soared with visions of victory. Then Daniel just kept running as if he was jogging the mile instead of playing kickball. Head down, he galumphed toward second, right into the waiting arms of the second-baseman who by now was holding the bouncy red ball. I think I cussed. Following the lead of their captain, my entire team started hurling verbal abuse at Daniel, who trotted toward home plate as if nothing happened. Upon reaching the angry mob, Daniel looked up long enough to see me and several of his teammates throw him to the ground and start kicking him. Daniel's screams didn't dissuade us, but the recess bell did. We left Daniel on the ground covered in dust and scurried back to class.

Within five minutes, before the days of cell phones or security cams, Mrs. Dawson knew all. Four of us slumped in our chairs, desperately trying to avoid eye contact with this woman we admired, yet who now seemed to be suffocating us with a look of disbelief and disenchantment.

So by age ten, I knew I was a sinner. I couldn't even live up to my incredibly low self-imagined standards. When I first heard the message of Jesus' forgiveness, it resonated with my internal broken compass. When I read that...

"God made him who had no sin to be sin for us,
so that in him we might become the righteousness of God,"

I reasoned that God knew what I did and was speaking directly to me.

After travelling the world for the 40 years that followed, I discovered I wasn't the only one conflicted by the oppressive feeling of personal sin.

Upon my first expedition to the mountains of Kyrgyzstan , my fellow hikers and I stumbled onto a willow tree covered with multi-colored bows fashioned from torn cloth. I asked those more experienced in Central Asian customs the meaning and discovered that the Kyrgyz "cast their sins" on holy trees. Trees that grow near natural mountain springs of water are endowed with the ability to remove sin and bring good luck. I wondered if there was some ancient connection to the biblical reference of Galatians 3:13 -- cursed is everyone (or every piece of cloth) who hangs on a tree.

A few seasons later I saw Russians gather outside of the Eastern Orthodox church for a different ceremony of cleansing. Instead of tying bows on a tree, the devotees waited through the entire night for a priest to sprinkle some holy water upon them in order to push the "reset" button on sin as they entered into a new year of spiritual accounts with God.

Each year, during the holiday of Korban, the streets of Central Asia filled with herds of sheep, blood-stained sidewalks, and boiling pots of mutton. Muslims who recognize their need for forgiveness recount the story of Abraham, then sacrifice a sheep to cleanse the past year's sin and start anew. Meat from the sacrifice is offered to friends, relatives, and the poor – also soothing guilty consciences.

A neighbor's home in the Caucuses, however, produced the most unusual atonement ritual I've experienced first-hand. Uncle Ahmed and his wife lived one house down from us with their son Kamal and his young bride Maya. Uncle Ahmed and I regularly interacted over fence issues, downed utility lines, and fees for using the common sewer pipe which ran down the length of our street, then conveniently ended atop a small cliff, where the raw sewage spilled out then magically disappeared down the hill. Kamal, the only son, worked in a precarious job as an inspector for contraband on the border of Azerbaijan and Dagestan. What he really did is stand next to a road block all day and tell Chechen terrorists to surrender their trucks full of drugs and weapons – or not, depending on the price. Kamal confided in me that he always wondered if he would make it back from his work alive, or if his car would explode the next time he tried to start it. He had dreams of leaving it all and starting his own business selling pomegranate wine.

As a cultural Muslim, Kamal did the minimum to appease Allah for the sins of which he was aware. One way to do so was to obey cultural customs, which were all interpreted through the lens of Islam. On the day

Kamal invited me to his home for his son Aziz's circumcision party, I wasn't sure what I was getting into. Faithful Muslims in this part of the world circumcise boys at the age of four, then dress them in a red skirt during the healing period. What Westerner's would interpret as a permanently self-image-scarring ritual of shame, the boys of the Caucuses relished as a badge of honor. I spoke with several men who recounted the pride of wearing their red skirts out onto the playground, envied by their pre-school comrades.

When I entered Uncle Ahmed's courtyard, box of chocolates in hand, there stood Kamal, bent over three dead chickens, blood slowly expanding out over the concrete pavers. Kamal explained that the sacrifice of chickens would cover his sins and was especially necessary on such a holy occasion. He also bragged that while most good Muslims sacrifice one chicken, he was covering all his bases by going for three. I jokingly applauded his efforts and fished for a transition into the gospel as he ushered me into the crowded house filled with food, balloons, and laughter.

Our conversation evaporated as I was immediately taken upstairs to the male room and seated at an ornately set table full of uncles, cousins, and officiating Muslim clerics. We all made small talk and grabbed handfuls of dried fruit and nuts from the bowls in front of us while head-covered women intermittently came in and out of the room with various forms of salads. The jovial environment led me to believe that the unpleasantries of the actual operation had already taken place, but just as I placed a fork full of beet salad into my mouth, Kamal burst through the door with Aziz in his arms and one of his uncles by his side.

The men slid plates aside, pinned Aziz down to the dinner table and gave the priest the nod. Four-year-old Aziz, who had entered the room smiling, now realized something was awry and began screaming for mercy. Shiny tools of the craft emerged from the Muslim cleric's pocket while women outside the doors began screaming in response to Aziz's pleas. Within seconds, metal flashed, screams escalated, women barged through the door, and what looked like a small ring of sautéed red onion flicked off the knife blade in an arc and landed with a little plop on the edge of my salad plate. In the cacophony of feminine shrieks and masculine cheers, no one except me seemed to notice the final resting place of the discarded body part. I sensitively tried to make eye contact with anyone more experienced in the etiquette of such matters, but hugging, high-fiving, and a sobbing mother seemed to have arrested everyone's attention. Do I flick it off my plate onto the table with a utensil? Will someone ask for it as a sacred memento later if I somehow brush it onto the floor? Should I just wrap it in a napkin and act like nothing ever happened?

Well, I opted for the napkin. I had perfected this skill on several earlier cross-cultural occasions when being served inedible sheep parts, or globs of tail fat. This was, however, the first and last time I've had to perform the slight-of-hand with a human body part.

Although I'm grateful to Kamal and poor little Aziz for providing an unforgettable evening, I'm saddened that so many people have yet to find true comfort for the universally recognized need of forgiveness. Neither sheep, nor chickens, nor bows on a tree can pay the price to rid men and women of their besetting sins, because the value of an animal or a ribbon is not equal to that of a man or woman. The price required to forgive all the sins accumulated during the life of a human is the life of another sin-free human. And only an infinite sin-free human can forgive the sins of all humanity. Jesus was that infinite sin-free human who exchanged His own life for ours.

Forty of my fifty years on this planet have been spent reveling in the freedom and forgiveness which Jesus' sacrifice for me has secured, so it only makes sense to spend the rest of my days helping others find that same freedom and forgiveness that nothing other than Jesus can truly provide.

"When I kept silent, my bones wasted away through my
groaning all day long. For day and night your hand was heavy
on me; my strength was sapped as in the heat of summer. Then
I acknowledged my sin to you and did not cover up my iniquity.
I said, 'I will confess my transgressions to the LORD.'
And you forgave the guilt of my sin."
Ps 32:3-5

REFLECTION

1. Describe a time when you felt burdened by your own sin?

2. What practical difference does it make in your life now to know you are
forgiven?

3. Take time to list the names of three friends or relatives who haven't yet
experienced Christ's forgiveness. Pray for them throughout this week.

THE TEST

Day 23 – by Dan

"Examine yourselves to see whether you are in the faith; test yourselves.
Do you not realize that Christ Jesus is in you—
unless, of course, you fail the test?"
2 Cor 13:5

It's been almost 400 years since the Pilgrims ran into Plymouth Rock and set up the first American church and potluck Thanksgiving dinner. Since everyone in the then "new" New England went to church every Sunday, most everybody figured their kids were automatically on their way to heaven due to hours logged sitting in church pews. This chafed early American reformer Jonathan Edwards so much that he wrote entire books to delineate the evidences that determine if someone is a true Christian inside and out.

Centuries later something similar is bugging me. Like much of the growingly global world, the majority of my supervision as an organizational leader for a worldwide Christian ministry occurs at a distance. I spend hours each week on Skype, Facebook, various social media apps, and crummy old phone lines attempting to assess the spiritual state, relational health, and strategic effectiveness of people who lead teams of two to twenty multicultural Christian workers. I'm not so concerned whether these team leaders are real Christians. I'm relying on an extensive application process and track record of service to sort that out. The bigger question in my mind is, "How do I identify the undeniable marks of spiritual maturity?" since the future of our ministry and the health of entire teams depends on it. Is the person on the other end of this cellular connection 12,000 miles away the best fit to lead others into healthy Biblical maturity? Jonathan Edwards at least had the advantage of stopping by Elder Owen's farm to see if he was sacrificing small animals to pagan deities or selling moonshine out of his cellar. I'm stuck with a crackly voice in a foreign language saying,

"We gathered to study the Bible today," or was that, "We squandered Judy's money away"? What? Great. Who's Judy?

However, hope is not lost. What Jonathan Edwards took 382 pages to explain[viii], I think I've boiled down to one simple litmus test. The real indicator of whether someone is fit to lead others in Christian work is found in 1 Peter chapter 5.

All of you, clothe yourselves with humility toward one another, because,
"'God opposes the proud but shows favor to the humble.'
Humble yourselves, therefore, under God's mighty hand,
that he may lift you up in due time."
1 Peter 5:5-6

When I'm looking for a real marker of maturity, I ask, "Does this leader regularly humble himself or herself by asking forgiveness from the people they've offended?"

In my 25 years of ministry, I've seen people talk about spiritual maturity, give sermons on holiness, and lead projects that help hundreds of needy people. None of these impress me as much as the simple act of humbling oneself before a colleague or a spouse or a child and asking for forgiveness, even when there are justifiable reasons for the actions that caused the offense.

Since the beginning of our faith journey requires that we humble ourselves and ask forgiveness from God, it seems logical that the same action (now directed toward God and one another) would be required to grow into Christian maturity. Furthermore, Philippians chapter two calls us to have the same attitude as the one found in Christ – an attitude manifested through letting go of privilege, emptying oneself of position, and humble submission for the well-being of others. Asking someone else for forgiveness, especially a leader asking forgiveness from those he or she leads, may be the key indicator of this attitude of humility.

On one occasion several years ago, a colleague and I confronted Ferid, one of our ministry leaders, with some behaviors that were driving a wedge between himself and the other members of his leadership team.

Ferid was bold, talented, and used to taking charge when no one else was willing to step up. He regularly capitalized on new opportunities to move the ministry forward. About the time that Ferid was growing more confident in his leadership role and more accustomed to making quick decisions, our ministry made the shift to leadership teams as opposed to individual ministry directors. Ferid's independence and unilateral decision-making didn't resonate well with those who formed his leadership team. After more than a year of attempting to help Ferid embrace shared leadership, he persisted in neglecting to consult his team on important decisions, in particular, decisions involving finances. From Ferid's perspective, his behavior was completely justifiable. He had done the research, identified the needs of the ministry, and had executed his plans in a timely manner, which could not have happened if he had wasted time consulting with others and waiting on their input. The result was some forward movement in big projects, but also distrust and conflict among those who were supposed to execute those same projects.

By the time the conflict rose to our attention, emotions were high. Members of the leadership team teetered on the edge of resignation. Accusations of financial foul play darted back and forth in emails. Our HR director and I flew into Ferid's city to try to sort things out. I immediately invited Ferid to our hotel to hear his side of the story and to compose a game plan to move forward. Ferid presented somewhat justifiable reasoning to undergird his recent behavior, yet the fact remained that mutual trust between the other leaders and himself was plummeting. I suggested the following course of action:

"During tomorrow's meeting with the leadership team, begin by apologizing for your part in the existing conflict. Take ownership of insufficient communication and failing to create adequate environments for the team to weigh in on significant decisions. Then see if that breaks the ice to move toward reconciliation and rebuilding trust."

Ferid nodded as if he agreed, but something in his distant stare made me question whether he really concurred with the proposal.

The following day's meeting turned into a disaster. After a few formalities, Ferid started in on his "apologies" one team member at a time.

"I'm sorry you are so clueless that you don't understand my leadership style..." began his first confession. It deteriorated from there to the point where I stopped the meeting, pulled Ferid aside, and asked him to step out of the room and out of his leadership position. When it came to what I believe is the true test of spiritual maturity – having the attitude of Christ, who humbled Himself – Ferid didn't get a passing grade. He proved that although he may be capable of effectively leading an organization, he wasn't ready to lead others in Christ-likeness.

Yet on other occasions, I've seen believers much younger in their faith than Ferid pass the test with flying colors. During one five-year period of ministry, Dina and I operated a for-profit coffee shop as a context for shining the light of Christ into an otherwise darkened Muslim city. One Friday night behind the coffee bar, a new Christ-following barista named Elshad showed a lapse of judgment. While working the evening shift under a female manager named Aygun, Elshad gave a friend who had come into the shop some free food without permission. When Aygun confronted him, Elshad replied with defiance and defensiveness. "I don't answer to you, or to anyone here! Dan and Dina will never fire me, because I'm one of the only men working here, and they need me too much." Aygun stepped back in shock, not knowing how to respond in this male dominated Muslim society. Saturday morning she directed her inner angst to me amidst tears: "I can't work the same shifts with Elshad anymore. One of us needs to leave."

When Elshad showed up for work at 5:00 p.m. Saturday, I pulled him into the kitchen. I asked for his side of the story, which confirmed Aygun's words, although intertwined with half-hearted apologies.

When it came my turn to speak, I explained, "You have broken two of our company values outlined in your training and which we try to reinforce each week at staff meeting: honesty and service. Giving away food was dishonest, but your lack of servant's attitude toward Aygun is an even bigger concern. We believe this work and workplace is a context for expressing the values of God's kingdom. You have two weeks to remedy the situation, because I can't have employees who don't embrace and apply our core values of honesty and service. You need to apologize to Aygun and out-serve the other employees on your shift for the next two weeks. I will interview them two weeks from Monday and we will reevaluate how things are going."

Monday evening Elshad asked for ten minutes of time at our all-employee staff meeting. I thought, *This is it; the turning point in Elshad's character development. Either he will stand up, defend his actions and separate himself from his believing colleagues and accountability structure, or he will humble himself, allow this work context to shape his character, and take a significant step in his spiritual growth.* I had no idea which way it would go.

As Elshad opened his mouth in front of his twelve co-workers, most of whom were women, and several of whom were Muslims, his face turned red. He choked out the words, "I was wrong. I've been prideful and selfish, and the other night I told Aygun that I don't need her or this job. I've realized that I do need all of you. You are my family, and I need you to tell me when I am in the wrong. I'm sorry." Half the employees in the room sat with dropped-jaws, the other half with teary eyes. This was the Holy Spirit's life-changing power on display for Christians and Muslims alike to gaze at in wonder. God had called Elshad into the examination room, and he walked out with academic honors.

Time and knowledge, while vital, are not the sole determiners of spiritual growth. As I lead from a distance, I've also called into question the reliability of ministry reports and correct answers during coaching calls. However, when I see a leader ask forgiveness from those he or she leads, and followers ask forgiveness from peers, it puts my heart at ease. Humility demonstrated through apology is an undeniable indicator that spiritual development is headed in the right direction.

That being said, I'd love to time-travel for a few days back to New England and pick Jonathan Edwards's brain on the subject. I suspect he would tell me that my "test" was relatively helpful but not quite as black and white as I assume. Maybe that's because Edwards got himself into trouble on a similar issue. After writing his treatise on the definitive signs of true conversion, Pastor Edwards applied it by serving communion only to those he believed demonstrated such signs. He was effectively run out of the church he pastored for 25 years and sent off into exile on the frontiers of the North American wilderness. Conclusion: Take any formula for seeing the unseen realities of the spiritual world with a grain of salt, and make sure we are applying what is clearly God's will in our own lives before dissecting the maturity of others.

> "Examine yourselves to see whether you are in the faith; test yourselves.
> Do you not realize that Christ Jesus is in you—
> unless, of course, you fail the test?"
> 2 Cor 13:5

REFLECTION

1. Is there any unresolved conflict in your life currently?

2. What is keeping you from taking the first step to reconcile the relationship?

3. Think through what it will cost you to apologize or ask someone you've offended for forgiveness. Now think of what it cost Jesus to forgive you. Are you willing to pay a small portion of what Jesus already paid for you?

CHOOSE THE MIDDLE SEAT
Day 24 - by Dan

> "At that time some Pharisees came to Jesus and said to him,
> "Leave this place and go somewhere else. Herod wants to kill
> you." He replied, "Go tell that fox, 'I will keep on driving out
> demons and healing people today and tomorrow, and on the
> third day I will reach my goal.' In any case, I must press on
> today and tomorrow and the next day—
> for surely no prophet can die outside Jerusalem!"
> Lk 13:31-33

Recently some neighbors and I formed a weekly group to discuss spiritual disciplines. After toying with a tiny bit of fasting, and a meager portion of solitude, we each committed to a week of study. Since I was already reading about the life of Jesus, I decided to look more intently at an obscure paragraph at the end of Luke chapter 13. As Jesus is on his merry way to Jerusalem with his disciples, some religious leaders kindly inform Jesus that King Herod was looking to kill him. Jesus dispassionately replies,

> "That's okay, I will just continue on my way to accomplish my purpose."
> (v.32 paraphrase)

In the verses that follow, Jesus makes it abundantly clear that he is fully aware of his imminent death, yet rather unflapped by it. Jesus shrugs off impending physical doom to pursue wholeheartedly the purpose for which God has placed him on earth.

Conveniently, my study of this passage coincided with a trip to a conference discussing God's global purposes for our generation. During the four days of meetings, 20 other global-minded Christian leaders and I were trying to digest a seemingly impossible vision of mobilizing 10 million men and women toward Christian influence by the year 2020. Those casting the vision had calculated that two committed influencers were needed to reach every 1000 people on the planet with the good news of Jesus. Since five billion people currently claim no affiliation with Christ, a little math and a lot of faith produced the 10 million-person goal. All of us in the room recognized that such an audacious proposition could only be fulfilled by a supernatural working of God, and the cooperation of hundreds of Christian organizations completely devoted to the God-given task. As the conference came to a close, I concluded that I could work the Luke 13 passage into a sermon with which to rally my tiny sphere of influence to accomplish a small piece of the audacious 10-million-by-2020 dream. The crux of my imagined message would be to embrace Jesus' "purpose versus self-preservation" prototype.

Tragically, my thesis was put to the test immediately upon leaving the conference. During my flight home I had hoped to get a little private time to compose the aforementioned masterpiece of self-sacrifice, but I was grossly inconvenienced by being assigned the middle seat for my overbooked five-hour journey. Comfortably utilizing my laptop turned out to be less than ideal with the limited elbow room and whatnot. So, for the entirety of the flight, I was relegated to talking with Steve the agnostic, who, despite his indifference toward the Almighty, had somehow conjured up enough divine favor to get the window seat. Steve seemed honestly interested in hearing how Jesus had changed my worldview as a teenager and continued His work of personal transformation 30 years later. He opened up about his struggles with marriage, divorce, and lasting happiness. When I proposed Jesus as the bedrock on which to construct the second half of his life, he made one of those sincere "huh" sounds, like he was really thinking about it. A few minutes later, Steve crawled over me to make his way to the bathroom, at which point Anna, the fortunate aisle passenger began to talk. Anna was a globally-minded believer who inadvertently eavesdropped on my conversation with Steve since we were huddled so closely together. She was encouraged at observing how retelling my abbreviated life story could transition naturally into a presentation of biblical truths and an explanation of the gospel message. Anna implied that she might try it on some friends of hers back home.

At some point in the conversations it occurred to me that the middle seat was an embodiment of the Luke 13 application point for my life. I can effectively double my chances of influencing others for Christ and fulfilling one of the main purposes of my existence by sitting in the middle seat. I'm only 5'10", so leg-room isn't a huge concern. I'm agile enough to maneuver over sleeping aisle passengers if nature calls. So the only reason I would choose an aisle or window would be to prioritize personal comfort over an eternal mandate. Yet when it comes to international travel, if given a choice between the middle seat or a nail through the hand, I would have to pause for a moment to decide. Nevertheless, Luke 13 did prompt me to ask, "What sacrifices might be required to see everyone in the world have an opportunity to know the God who created them and deeply loves them?"

In order to answer that question, I now need to refer to the more exemplary lives of others since my own life is conspicuously absent of sacrifice in light of a higher cause.

Andrew and Elaine moved to post-Soviet Muslim Central Asia in 1996 with four of their five children in tow. Andrew was possibly the most qualified person ever to join our organization, with several master's degrees, a Ph.D. in world religions from Harvard University, and twenty years of pastoral and church planting experience. Elaine was no less accomplished. Within a couple of years, their family was giving leadership to a network of church planters, training pastors, laying the groundwork to open a Bible school, and speaking fluent Russian.

On one ordinary evening four years into their overseas sojourn, Andrew and Elaine tucked their pre-teen daughters into bed and proceeded to collapse into a deep sleep, exhausted from attending to the endless needs of their adopted foreign community. In the dark morning hours, noises at the front door awoke the daughters who saw three masked figures standing at the threshold of their room, one holding a lighter, and all of them carrying hatchets. The men silently departed, closing the door behind them. Two of the men made their way into Andrew and Elaine's bedroom and commenced their plot of terror while the third paced outside the girls' room. The girls crawled out their window into the courtyard as the sleeping parents fell victim to the crushing initial blows from the blunt end of the hatchets.

Unlike Dolby-enhanced movies, the only sound was the cracking of bones followed by muffled groans and desperate calls upon the name of Jesus. After an agonizing series of unrelenting impacts, Andrew, shocked at remaining conscious, managed to wrest the hatchet from the hand of his attacker. Whether in answer to prayer, or part of an original plan to stop short of murder, the masked men chose to flee. Andrew, fearing his daughters had been abducted, struggled into the back garden where he found the terrified girls hiding and immediately secured them with a neighbor. He then rushed back in to the crime-scene to find Elaine on the floor with a cracked skull, broken bones, and bleeding from the ears. A painstakingly slow medical evacuation ensued, followed by surgery, rehabilitation, and a litany of pleas from friends and family never to return to that hell on earth.

Nevertheless, like Jesus, Andrew and Elaine had already counted the cost of fulfilling God's call. They knew if those people were to hear about the love of Jesus, someone would have to make sacrifices. When they did return, their new friends listened with fresh ears and responded with renewed zeal. Church planting efforts multiplied, and Andrew seized opportunities to mobilize scores of men and women to meet the growing needs of post 9/11 war-ravaged neighborhoods. Today, Andrew and Elaine continue to provide leadership for thousands involved in getting the message of Jesus's love out to the remaining five billion who have never clearly heard.

In light of those who have really obeyed Jesus's command to leave all and follow Him, my puny middle-seat sacrifice seems pathetic. Likewise, I wager that most of us mortals deal with similarly meager choices in our journey to take up our cross and follow him.

Choosing to wait for marriage before having sex, refusing to lie even a little bit on your taxes, or giving away a percentage of your income may be your uncomfortable middle seat.

For me, I fly almost every month, and usually for 12 to 14 hours at a whack, so the middle seat is my middle seat. As painful and visceral as agreeing with God and disregarding personal preservation may seem, I've tried it. The level of pain I feel when choosing the middle seems to be a gauge of my progress in liberation from self-absorption. I have to admit that most often personal preservation wins, but every once in a while, I actually do it. I move myself into a middle seat. And most times God provides wonderful conversations with people who encourage me more than I them.

> "At that time some Pharisees came to Jesus and said to him, "Leave this place and go somewhere else. Herod wants to kill you." He replied, "Go tell that fox, 'I will keep on driving out demons and healing people today and tomorrow, and on the third day I will reach my goal.' In any case, I must press on today and tomorrow and the next day—for surely no prophet can die outside Jerusalem!"
> Lk 13:31-33

REFLECTION

1. Where are you choosing comfort over obedience?

2. What do you think needs to be sacrificed in order to make progress in your relationship with God?

3. How might the benefits of a deeper relationship with God outweigh the sacrifices?

WAITING FOR THE BLUE ZONE
Day 25 – by Dan

> "But I am hard-pressed from both directions, having the desire
> to depart and be with Christ, for that is very much better; yet to
> remain on in the flesh is more necessary for your sake.
> Convinced of this, I know that I will remain and continue with
> you all for your progress and joy in the faith,"
> Phil 1:23-35

When I was a kid, I dreamed of being a stuntman. Jumping off
buildings and riding a wheelie on a motorcycle out of the rubble of a
burning building would be the ultimate job. I couldn't wait to grow up and
do all the stuff that makes life exciting. What I never dreamed of as a kid
was sitting around the grown-up dinner table talking about assisted-care
living, dementia, cremation, and cancer treatments. Fortunately, most of
these topics don't relate directly to me yet (although my wife might
disagree on the assisted-care part), but it seems that people all around me
are now facing such topics themselves or with loved ones.

The paradox, however, is that despite the not-so-exciting realities of
the grown-up world, we all seem to be strategizing about how to live
longer and safer. A recent book called *The Blue Zones* recites,
"extraordinary accounts of the oldest people on the planet...and... how to
incorporate these powerful lifestyle characteristics into your daily routine so
that you, too, can live into your Blue Zone"[ix] (i.e. really old).

Really? Do I really want to live to be an ailment-filled 100+ year-old,
when I could be spending that extra 25 years that I've "cheated death" in
the thrill-inspiring presence of Jesus my savior? It seems to me that the
centenarians are the ones who have been "cheated" out of a score of face-
time with the Lord.

I think the root issue may be a bit deeper. Due to the advances in
medicine, technology, and ice cream flavors, we who live in countries
developed enough to visit Cold Stone Creamery[R] on our way home from

outpatient orthoscopic surgery have come to believe this planet is our true home. We snuggle up next to our wireless electronic device with seasonal warm or cool air blowing over our fuzzy slippers and think, *this is what life is all about.* But to paraphrase the Apostle Paul in Philippians 1:21-24, "It would be way better to go be with Jesus, but if God still wants me to be of use to Him here, I guess I'll have to stick around on earth."

Paul seems to make it abundantly clear that benefiting others in the service of Christ is *THE* reason God sustained my life today, and may or may not continue to do so tomorrow.

Two years ago, Jason, one of our colleagues working to get the good news of Jesus out to unreached people in a Muslim country, became the focus of our crisis management team. Jason was leading a home church with a dozen local formerly Muslim men, when a terrorist group blew open his front gate with grenades attached to a suicide bomber. Three more extremists rushed into the courtyard with machine guns. After shooting the guards, they broke through the front door, and opened fire on Jason and his two teenage children. All three were ushered into Jesus' presence that day. During the weeks that followed, we evacuated all our foreign workers from that country and relocated our national staff to relatively safer venues. I also began asking God and others what He was doing through this tragedy.

Answers were slow in coming, but an unexpected conversation began to shed a bit of perspective on Jason's homegoing. Prompted by a newspaper photo of a local surfboard with a shark bite taken out of it, I asked my high school boys, "What do you think would be the worst way to die?" After several minutes of cycling through the usual answers of Great White Shark attack, fire ants, and a zombie apocalypse, the conversation took an unexpected turn. Out of the blue, I asked, "What do you think would be the *best* way to die?"

Just the question itself seemed to clarify the issue at hand. We are all going to die. "It is appointed for men to die once and after this comes judgment," says the book of Hebrews. Whether at age 17 or 107, we are all passing from this temporary dwelling into something more permanent. Mathematically speaking 17 divided by infinity and 107 divided by infinity both equal zero. That means the number of years we survive on this planet is only as valuable as the amount of eternally significant activity which fills those years. Paul had it right when he said, "To depart and be with Christ is very much better; yet to remain on in the flesh is more necessary for your sake." Paul saw serving others as his reason for remaining temporarily separated from his true love – Jesus.

"What do you think would be the best way to die?" also calls into question the prevailing Western notion that this life is the "real" one, and eternal life is some altered state of cosmic being which will be nice, but not that exciting. Most Western Christians wouldn't admit we think that way, but the culture we live in apparently thinks so. Why else would we want to stretch this "real" life out into the 100s. Why would we make movies about bucket lists, and write books about *1000 Places to Visit Before You Die?* The only conclusion is that we believe we need to fit all the good stuff into this lifetime because the life to come isn't that great. Jesus taught otherwise.

Jesus is our only example of what our heavenly state will look like. Others whom Jesus brought back from the dead did not have resurrection bodies. They came back to life in their flawed, aging, earthly bodies just to die again at a later date. Old Testament figures such as Enoch just disappeared into heaven without dying, so he wasn't much help in giving us an eternal snapshot of life on the other side. But Jesus came back to life in an eternal body. His new body was different enough from the pre-crucifixion model that most people didn't recognize him (Jn 20:14), yet similar enough that once he engaged friends in conversation, they knew who He was (Jn 20:16). His new body could pass through walls (Jn 20:19) and seemingly appear and disappear at will (Lk 24:31). Most significantly, the ressurrected Jesus had a real body that was touchable (Lk 24:39), enjoyed food (Lk 24:41), and engaged in relationship (Lk 24:32).

You and I will spend eternity in similar bodies, bodies that eat and drink and enjoy friendships. Our bodies will recognize each other, yet be free from some boundaries (like walls and doors) that currently separate friends. The next life is more real than this one, more permanent, more reliable, and more filled with joy. This truth frees us to expend this earthly life on meeting the needs of others instead of trying to check off the boxes on our own "must do, must see" list. Just like Paul, knowing the wonderful reality of our future bodies motivates us to live on in the flesh, not because it is better, but because it is more necessary for others' sake.

According to Dietrich Bonhoeffer, "Death is only dreadful for those who live in dread and fear of it. Death is grace, the greatest gift of grace that God gives people who believe in him...It beckons to us with heavenly power, if only we realize that it is the gateway to our homeland, the tabernacle of joy, the everlasting kingdom of peace."[x]

Jesus, the Apostle Paul, and Bonhoeffer all seem to agree. We need not hedge our lives in safety hoping to make it into the "Blue Zone", nor feverishly pursue adventures on some bucket list. The best is yet to come, so invest this brief vapor of a lifetime in serving others for Jesus's sake.

Back to the question, "What would be the best way to die?" As I've pondered this, I've often thought of Jason. When I visited Jason's ministry location a few years ago, I stopped by a school that provides remedial education for street-children. For a few minutes I sat next to a beautifully frail tiny head-scarved eight-year-old girl whom I imagined being kicked around the city's dusty streets if she weren't sitting in class next to me. I wondered how those same streets would treat her when she turned into a beautiful 16-year-old woman. I was glad those who helped start the school valued her well-being above sliding safely into their Blue Zone.

Jason exuded passion to teach God's word to those who had no opportunity to hear otherwise. He had moved his family to the hardest of the hard places because He was convinced God wanted to reach all the nations with the love of Christ and because of the joy he himself experienced by seeing hopeless lives instilled with new purpose and peace. Then one day, in the midst of doing what he loved most, and in the center of God's will for his life, someone came into the room and turned out the lights. Maybe that is the best way to die. If Jason could have engineered his life and death, my guess is that he may not have changed a thing. Would he have wanted more time with his children? They are together in heaven for all eternity eating and laughing and loving each other in real resurrection bodies. Would he have wanted his wife to be with him? She remains on in the flesh, serving others and storing up even more eternal rewards.

Having now an eternal perspective, Jason might echo the worlds of Bishop J C Ryle in his commentary on a parable in Mark chapter 4:

> "No farmer thinks of cutting his wheat when it is green... God deals with His work of grace exactly in the same way. He never removes His people from this world till they are ripe and ready... They never die at the wrong time, however mysterious their deaths appear sometimes to man... Let us rest satisfied, that there is no chance, no accident, no mistake about the decease of any of God's children."[xi]

What would Jason have changed about his life and death? Maybe he would simply stop back by and remind us that to depart and be with Christ is very much better.

> "I am hard-pressed from both directions, having the desire to depart and be with Christ, for that is very much better; yet to remain on in the flesh is more necessary for your sake. Convinced of this, I know that I will remain and continue with you all for your progress and joy in the faith,"
> Phil 1:23-35

REFLECTION

1. Is there any area of your life where fear is keeping you from following God whole-heartedly?

2. Take some time to identify specifically what you are afraid of?

3. If heaven is real, and we will spend all eternity with our loved ones, and with the One who loves us best, what fears are actually lies you are believing?

PARASITES AND MEDIOCRITY
Day 26 – by Dan

> "Yes, everything else is worthless when compared with the
> infinite value of knowing Christ Jesus my Lord. For his sake I
> have discarded everything else, counting it all as garbage, so
> that I could gain Christ and become one with him. I no longer
> count on my own righteousness through obeying the law;
> rather, I become righteous through faith in Christ. For God's
> way of making us right with himself depends on faith."
> Phil 3:8-9

"I'm afraid of parasites crawling into my head at night and eating my brain. What are you afraid of?" chirped my son Levi from the back seat. Thus went the banter in the carpool of 14-year-old boys. After several humbling instances, I've learned that Levi probably knows more about life than I do, so I pondered the parasite threat for a moment. Thankfully, I recalled an account from a book by a brain surgeon who documented an episode with a patient from the hills of Kentucky. This man had a head injury that he never bothered to fuss with, so maggots got into his skull and actually ate part of his brain. The ironic part is that the parasites were eating away the infected flesh, thus slowing the spread of the infection, and serendipitously saving the old guy's life.[xii] When I relayed the story to my backseat vermiphobes, they were somewhat comforted.

Having swiftly disposed of Levi's fear, I decided to tackle my own greatest horror -- living a life of mediocrity. I'm afraid of blending into the crowd, getting consumed with my own petty aspirations and missing a life of great significance and service to others. As one author noted, I'm afraid of failing at things that matter, and even more afraid of succeeding at things that don't matter.[xiii]

It could be that my mediocrity dilemma is simply comparison. On days when I surround myself with other underachievers shopping for fishing gear in Walmart at 2:00 p.m. on a Wednesday afternoon, I feel pretty good. Conversely, I once walked with my son around the campus of Stanford University listening to the 21-year-old genius-turned-tour-guide skim through the seemingly endless list of Stanford-grad achievements. I immediately wanted to take a nap to underscore my lifetime of insignificance.

Where does all this comparison and need to feel special originate? Sociologist/vulnerability expert Brene Brown blames the information age. The Internet constantly bombards us with videos and hyperlinks of people who are better than we are at everything we could ever imagine doing.[xiv] Sherwood Lingenfelter, professor of intercultural studies at Biola University, believes it goes even deeper, to the root of culture itself. According to the professor, "culture is created ... to maintain social control through its rules, norms, and sanctions for behavior."[xv] In some cultures, social control is exerted through fear of the opinions and approval of others in the community. So maybe my fear of mediocrity is just a preoccupation with what others think about me. Although this seems like a minor issue on the surface, I've had the privilege of observing what the fear of social opinion can do if left unchecked.

Central Asia is teeming with societal pressures from anonymous onlookers. It starts with the need to polish your shoes daily to be respectable, refraining from sitting on concrete to maintain your fertility, and never leaving home with wet hair to save your reputation. And it ends with wife-stealing.

Janny was a sophomore at the Agricultural Institute when we met her. She distinguished herself from the other female students by her refusal to flaunt the knee-high leather boots and fur-collared overcoats. She preferred basketball and t-shirts and had no problem working her way into a game of 3-on-3 streetball with the boys. This may not seem odd to Westerners, but in a Muslim culture of clearly demarcated masculine and feminine behaviors, Janny was an anomaly.

Janny's separation from the norms of society only grew after meeting some semi-pro basketball players who shared how Jesus had changed their lives. Shortly thereafter, she too decided to become a follower of Jesus in a country full of Muslims.

Dina spent the next several months studying the Bible with Janny and other women from Bishkek's Agricultural Institute. Then one week Janny didn't show. None of the other girls knew of her whereabouts, yet no one was overly concerned. But three weeks without any Janny sightings caused suspicions to rise. When Dina expressed her concerns, the girls from the Bible study started to unpack the culturally-accepted dynamics of Central-Asian wife-stealing.

When a man from this part of the world decides it's time to get married, he conspires with friends and family to obtain a bride. The potential groom and his posse of buddies then roam the streets of their village or city looking for an unsuspecting female of marrying age. Once they zero-in on any relatively attractive stranger of the opposite sex, the band of males abduct the woman, take her to the groom's home, hold her hostage overnight, and the marriage is official. Once the woman has spent the night at the man's home, whether they sleep together or not, society considers her married or defiled.

Public shaming prevents her parents from taking her back into their home, even if she asks to return. If she runs away, society labels her tarnished and unfit to marry again. Since Central Asian culture views a woman's sole purpose for existence as bearing children, running away from this unknown husband means no marriage, no children, and no reason for being. So, the stolen bride's choices were few -- remain with the stranger or become a social outcast without family or future. Janny, the one who didn't care what others thought, had fallen prey to a culture controlled by what others thought.

Three months after the day she disappeared, Janny managed to locate a pay phone in the remote village where she was being held. She probed Dina about the biblical view of divorce, birth control, and God's plan for her life. Dina attempted to help Janny navigate these deep theological waters but had trouble giving black and white answers in a cross-cultural mire. God would have to step in to lead this new believer down the particular path He had engineered for her.

Another three months passed before Janny called again to announce her escape, emancipation, and exodus to a neighboring city where she asked if she could sign on as a volunteer with one of our ministry teams. By doing so, she effectively sacrificed her chances of re-marrying, having children, or ever being seen as an honorable woman within her culture. In addition, Janny would always have to wrestle with what God thought about her "divorcing" a man she never agreed to "marry." Janny began a do-over to redeem the lost year of her life, but in doing so, she also set a course that placed complete dependence upon Jesus to meet significant relational needs for the rest of her life.

Janny continues in ministry as a part of a national leadership team. Still unmarried, yet loving Jesus, she counsels women in her culture to find their worth in God alone. She also models for me how to overcome my insignificant mediocrity fears – by rejecting the opinions of men and embracing the realities of God...

"Therefore, since we have been made right in God's sight by faith, we have peace..." (Rom 5:1a)

Daily rumination on the truth that I am right with the God of the universe supersedes any need to be exalted in the eyes of peers, parents, or Facebook friends. I've already been exalted to the heavenly places because of Christ's love and sacrifice for me. (Eph 2:6) There is no higher position to attain.

Forty years from now, I may wake up and realize I was never as great in the eyes of the world as Leonardo da Vinci, or Shaun White, or Bono. But 140 years from now, the only thing everyone will be talking about is how great Jesus is. So why let the fear of mediocrity steal today's joy of the eternal righteousness imparted to us through Jesus?

"Yes, everything else is worthless when compared with the infinite value of knowing Christ Jesus my Lord. For his sake I have discarded everything else, counting it all as garbage, so that I could gain Christ and become one with him. I no longer count on my own righteousness through obeying the law; rather, I become righteous through faith in Christ. For God's way of making us right with himself depends on faith."
Phil 3:8-9

REFLECTION

1. Whose opinions typically drive your behavior or aspirations?

2. If pleasing God was the primary determining factor in your decision making, what behaviors would change?

3. What would be the best compliment someone might say about you at your own funeral? Are you investing in that aspect of your life?

I STILL HAVEN'T FOUND WHAT I'M LOOKING FOR
Day 27 – by Dan

"Let us think of ways to motivate one another
to acts of love and good works."
Heb 10:24

Recently I've been looking for something I can't find. A few years ago I stepped into a job overseeing approximately 330 people organized into about 50 teams spread across 10 countries. Thus, I have an ever-growing need to find sharp, godly, mature leaders who ideally think just as I do about all the important topics in life, but surpass me in charm, passion, and people skills. It would be nice if they played the guitar or cello as well. I need only a handful of such leaders to guide our organization into a glorious future, with myself at the helm humbly refusing to take any credit for the success along the way.

This morning I woke up and realized that I have unconsciously fallen prey to the same fatal flaw Marx and Lenin made a century ago - discounting the biblical truth that people really do have a sinful nature, and dreaming that if everyone is given a couple of loaves of bread and a rusty factory to go to from 9 a.m. to 5 p.m., they would all be happy and play well together. Unfortunately, all my real-life comrades seem periodically to argue, complain, disagree with my inspired direction, and pound the table with their shoe. I don't like that part.

I think psychologists call this a good/bad split: a false view that people are all good or all bad instead of a combination of both. It turns out there are no people among my sphere of acquaintances who don't have a few annoying tendencies. Hamo in Armenia is a strategic thinker and detailed manager, yet given to outbursts of anger. Nurlan in Kyrgyzstan is magnetic with people and exudes joy wherever he goes, yet can't return an email if his life depended on it. Zia in Kazakhstan can mobilize hundreds of others to accomplish feats of greatness, yet seems

151

continually derailed by mismanagement of personal finances. Maybe these shortcomings bother me all the more because they are pieces of me.

Therefore, I've realized I need a new strategy to lead the people under my care -- people created in God's image with talents, great ideas, and a few "service items" (which seems to be the new in-flight term for "trash").

Fortunately, not long ago I came across a podcast where a church leader was interviewing the former CEO of Home Depot. When asked about his secrets of success, the CEO immediately highlighted a key activity that consumed a significant portion of his time – hand written "thank you" notes. In fact, this boss of 330,000 employees wrote 100 thank you notes by hand each week.[xvi]

I immediately hit the rewind button on my phone to make sure I heard that correctly, while doing a few calculations in my mind. One hundred thank you notes. Assuming a five-day work week, that means 20 notes per day, every day. Given a minimum writing time of three minutes per note, that still equals one hour every day of the week, every week of the year, scribbling out niceties onto corporate stationery. Furthermore, someone had to identify who the worthy recipients were, fold the paper, put the note in the envelope, address that envelope, lick and stick the stamp, and drive them to the post office (which was probably another 45 minutes per day). Surely the leader of 330,000 people had a few other urgent items on his agenda and lots of problems to solve, not to mention the pressure of selling a zillion dollars' worth of merchandise to satisfy investors. Nonetheless, Home Depot sales increased significantly during this CEOs tenure, and employees ended up framing the 'presidential thank-you notes' as badges of honor. Maybe the CEO of Home Depot is smarter than I am.

Upon further reflection, I realized that this CEO was not only putting into practice the biblical principle described in Hebrews 10:24, but reinforcing organizational values, demonstrating member care, and building a reserve of employer-employee trust through his seemingly insignificant act of recognizing people for doing the right things. Could there be anything more important for the long-term health of an organization than that? He *is* smarter than I am. But, I'm smart enough to steal his idea and implement it in our organization as well.

So, this past year, in addition to recognizing that our best people are still a mix of awesome and awful, our leadership team has chosen to focus on the bright spots and recognize the individuals who make marvelous things happen in our organization. We're taking our cues from Home Depot and weekly recording how many of our staff we can bolster with words of affirmation for jobs well done.

Taking this concept of a good/bad split one step further, it also dawned on me that I need to embrace the reality of both ideal and appalling in myself. My disappointment with my rogue thoughts, self-centeredness, and apathy invokes fits of defensiveness and jealousy. I shy away from others whom I imagine to be all good, and ask myself, "What could I possibly contribute to their lives, since I'm such a mess?" My unbiblical view of human nature (seeing others as all good or bad or better or worse than myself) undermines my proactivity to engage with the needs of my peers, subordinates, superiors, and the world.

We are made a little lower than the angels (Ps 8:5) yet fall short of the glory of God at every turn (Rom 3:23). We really are humorous, disappointing, and compassion-inspiring blends of triviality, malice, and magnificence. So, I'm asking God to help me believe Romans 3:23 and implement Hebrews 10:24.

What am I really looking for in my search for the perfect coworker? -- probably flawed people like me who need ample doses of encouragement, inspiration, and a sputnik (which in Russian means someone to come along for the journey). Combine those types of people with a few hundred thank you notes and I may find what I'm looking for.

"Let us think of ways to motivate one another
to acts of love and good works."
Heb 10:24

REFLECTION

1. How do you reconcile the biblical truths that people are created in God's image, worth of Christ's life, yet sinful and selfish without exception?

2. How can you encourage someone toward love and good deeds today?

3. If God were to write you a thank you note, what would He say?

THE TREASURE

Day 28 – by Dan

"I will praise the LORD, who counsels me; even at night my heart instructs me... You make known to me the path of life; you will fill me with joy in your presence, with eternal pleasures at your right hand."
Ps 16:7,11

When I moved from sunny California to Central Asia 20+ years ago, I expected to be stretched a bit, and even relished the "growth opportunity." What I didn't expect was 11 people in my house from 6 a.m. to 10 p.m. using the single "team" computer to send messages through a strange new medium called e-mail. In addition to the homesick Americans, 15-20 local college students from the neighboring university dropped by daily unannounced to spend time with the new foreigners in town.

One spring day my wife and I realized our hospitality envelope had exceeded capacity when we glanced out our window to see a familiar family walking through the courtyard toward our fifth-floor apartment. In unison, we immediately turned off the lights, bolted the front door and threw ourselves down on the living room floor. We kept completely silent during the seemingly endless knocking and ringing of the doorbell. Then to our relief, a concert of footsteps faded off down the echoing concrete stairwell.

Letting several more minutes pass for safe measure, I army-crawled over to the window and peered into the courtyard, only to find that the family had parked itself on a bench adjacent to our building's only entrance/exit. We were now trapped in our self-made prison cell until darkness drove the invaders back to their own territory.

This event, and several others like it in those early years, forced me regularly to evaluate my calling, priorities, and limits of relational energy. Life was so full of people, activities, and events, I needed simplification. "Is this a task only I can do, or can it be delegated to others?" This question became my daily mantra. Even among the tasks only

I could do, I needed to focus on what produced the greatest results with the least amount of resources expended.

It turns out several clever (and probably overwhelmed) individuals surfaced this dilemma long before I did. Vilfredo Pereto back in 1900 called it the 80/20 principle: 20% of expended effort tends to produce 80% of the results, while 80% of activity is effectually wasted on producing only 20% of outcomes.[xvii]

Two decades after Central Asia's butt-whooping, I've reopened the 80/20 discussion with coworkers. Now juggling a multinational organization with never-ending needs, requests, successes, and conflicts, I'm still digging for the elusive 20% of leverage activities that will produce 80% of desired results. This week's hunt unearthed treasure.

The guest speaker at church last Sunday claimed that, "Who we are inside determines what we see, and what we see determines what we do." My meditation on this pithy phrase quickly led to an afternoon nap, but when I awoke I perused an article by John Ortberg given to me in a completely disconnected context by an unrelated source. With a feeling that someone was stalking me, I read Ortberg's almost identical observation. "As we spend time with God, we will see what God sees."[xviii] I attributed the coincidence to God and figured He was trying to get my attention.

My elementary synopsis of the "80/20," "seeing," and "spending time with God" message is this: As we spend time with God in prayer, reading, strolling in nature, or dialoguing with Him in the car, we give God the opportunity to impart to us ideas. Psalm 16 claims that it is God who counsels us and even instructs us during our sleep. Ideas imparted from God illuminate the best paths in life, because God's ideas, as they percolate in our minds, help us see the world and people as God sees them. We see our teenage daughter's conflict with friends as opportunities to teach kindness, initiative, and unconditional love. We see looming college expenses as hopeful soil for God to grow a new miracle. We see unfulfilled dreams as springboards to discover greater satisfaction in God's immediate ocean of joy. We see traffic as an advanced course in patience and a chance to ponder what we are hurrying off to anyway.

156

Many of us in this information age no longer make our money digging holes with shovels or pulling metal out of a furnace with giant tongs. Rather, we exchange ideas. We may use words or texts or pictures, but the commodity we are trading is ideas. Those ideas shape our decisions and actions and eventually our destinies. Therefore, the most valuable "activity" in this week's schedule may be non-activity. If we stop and sit in God's presence, He may pass on the treasure of ideas. Ideas may come through the Bible or a sermon or a quiet inner voice and set the course for a glorious future.

C.S. Lewis noted, "If you read history, you will find that the Christians who did the most for the present world were precisely those who thought most of the next. It is since Christians have largely ceased to think of the other world that they have become so ineffective in this."[xix]

Is there anything more essential in my daily schedule than being with God, receiving his counsel, and thinking His thoughts in order to accomplish what is truly significant? I'm convinced that a large portion of the 20% leverage activity for any situation is to align our ideas with God's ideas. This stopping, pausing, connecting with God, and thinking is not just for ministers and popes, but for all of us. Because, like it or not, ideas will determine what we do next. God's ideas will allow us to see what next step is the best next step.

"I will praise the LORD, who counsels me; even at night my heart instructs me... You make known to me the path of life; you will fill me with joy in your presence, with eternal pleasures at your right hand."
Ps 16:7,11

REFLECTION

1. What new ideas has God given you this month?

2. When will you set aside time to allow God to give you His ideas?

3. In addition to the Bible, what resources might give valuable ideas to shape a God-honoring life?

ENDNOTES

[i] Paraphrase taken from Timothy Keller's blog: Keller Project: "I was not raised to do such a thing!" August 18, 2009 https://lukewoodhouse.wordpress.com/category/tim-keller/

[ii] A.W. Tozer, *The Knowledge of the Holy.* Harper Collins, New York, 1961. p.1.

[iii] Os Guiness, *The Call.* Thomas Nelson, Nashville TN, 1998. p.24.

[iv] Aaron Neville, Rob Matthes. Universal Music Publishing Group.

[v] Finishing The Task website: http://www.finishingthetask.com/uupgs.php?sort=Country

[vi] Daniel Goleman, *Primal Leadership.* Harvard Business School, Boston, MA, 2002. p.8.

[vii] Karl Marx, *Deutsch–Französische Jahrbücher.* 1844. Introduction.

[viii] Jonathan Edwards, *The Religious Affections.* Banner of Truth Trust, Edinburgh, 1961.

[ix] Dan Buettner, *The Blue Zones.* National Geographic, Memphis, TN, 2012. Jacket.

[x] Eric Metaxas, *Bonhoeffer: Pastor, Martyr, Prophet, Spy.* Thomas Nelson, Nashville, TN, 2010. p. 531.

[xi] J. C. Ryle, *Expository Thoughts on Mark.* Banner of Truth Trust, Edinburgh, 1985. p. 76.

[xii] Katrina Firlik, *Another Day in the Frontal Lobe.* Random House, New York, 2007.

[xiii] Bob Goff, *Love Does.* Thomas Nelson, Nashville, TN, 2012. p.30.

[xiv] Brene Brown, *Daring Greatly.* Avery, NY, 2012. p.23.

[xv] Sherwood Lingenfelter, *Transforming Culture.* Baker Books, Grand Rapids, MI, 1998. p.17.

[xvi] Andy Stanley Leadership Podcast, https://itunes.apple.com/us/podcast/andy-stanley-leadership-podcast/id290055666?mt=2 Vision: A Conversation with Frank Blake - Part 1

[xvii] Richard Koch, *The 80/20 Principle.* Crown Publishing, New York, 1998. p.6.

[xviii] John Ortberg, *Soul Keeping.* Zondervan, Grand Rapids, MI, 2014. p. 134.

[xix] C.S Lewis, *Mere Christianity,* Harper, San Francisco, CA 2001. p. 18.

ABOUT THE AUTHORS

Dan and Dina Krull believe that each of us can contribute to God's magnificent purposes for human history. Their contribution happened to take the form of education, relief, and business initiatives in the Muslim world.

After receiving their bachelor's degrees from Colorado State University and the University of California at Santa Barbara respectively, Dan and Dina entered full-time service with CRU, an international Christian ministry.

In 1994, the Krulls moved to Central Asia where they led multiple teams throughout the developing country of Kyrgyzstan. During this season, both Dan and Dina completed a Master's degree in organizational leadership from Azusa Pacific University.

After ten years in Kyrgyzstan, Dan and Dina transferred ministry leadership to a team of indigenous believers and moved with their four children to another Islamic country north of Iran. There, the Krulls along with a team of wonderful staff and partners created self-sustaining businesses to reflect God's kingdom principles in a corrupt economic and political climate.

After completing a Doctor of Ministry degree in 2011, Dan took a regional leadership role with CRU to provide supervision of 50 ministry teams in Persia, Armenia, Central Asia and Turkey.

Together Dan, Dina, and their four children enjoy cycling, surfing, tennis, nature, and good coffee. Their love for laughter and learning are reflected in these accounts of their journey on the Silk Road. May their comic confessions remind readers that God can use ordinary people to promote His purposes.

Levi   Krissy   Ellie   Dina   Dan   Jack

THE KRULLS

For additional copies of *Road Scholars*
please look on amazon.com
or contact Dan and Dina Krull at

ddkrull@securenym.net